MOTIVATION, BELIEFS, AND ORGANIZATIONAL TRANSFORMATION

MOTIVATION, BELIEFS, AND ORGANIZATIONAL TRANSFORMATION

Thad B. Green and Raymond T. Butkus

Q

QUORUM BOOKS
Westport, Connecticut • London

Library of Congress Cataloging-in-Publication Data

Green, Thad B.
    Motivation, beliefs, and organizational transformation / Thad
    B. Green & Raymond T. Butkus.
        p.   cm.
    Includes bibliographical references and index.
    ISBN 1–56720–282–9 (alk. paper)
    1. Employee motivation.   2. Organizational change.   I. Butkus,
    Raymond T.   II. Title.
    HF5549.5.M63G747   1999
    658.3'14—dc21   98–51660

British Library Cataloguing in Publication Data is available.

Library of Congress Catalog Card Number: 98–51660
ISBN: 1–56720–282–9

First published in 1999

Quorum Books, 88 Post Road West, Westport, CT 06881
An imprint of Greenwood Publishing Group, Inc.
www.quorumbooks.com

Printed in the United States of America

The paper used in this book complies with the
Permanent Paper Standard issued by the National
Information Standards Organization (Z39.48–1984).

10 9 8 7 6 5 4 3 2 1

Contents

Preface

Improving motivation at work in order to better manage organizational change is the central topic of this book, which was the joint effort of two people: Thad Green, who developed the change model called the "belief system of motivation and performance," and Raymond Butkus, a longtime AT&T executive who initiated and managed the most extensive application of the belief system.

The change model that you will read about in this book is entirely my own creation, but it evolved from the research of a long line of thinkers in the twentieth century who focused on the issue of motivation at work. Among them, the one who had the greatest influence on me was Victor Vroom. A prominent figure in the academic world during the 1960s and 1970s, Vroom was a psychologist who taught at a number of prestigious schools during his career, including the Carnegie Institute of Technology and Yale University. One early book of his, *Work and Motivation,* published in 1964, is now considered a seminal work in the field of organizational psychology.

Vroom was one of the chief proponents of what has become known as the "expectancy theory" of motivation. I was never a student of Vroom's, nor did I read his books while I was at school. In fact, it wasn't until 1977, at the tail end of my own career as a professor of management, that I first learned about Victor Vroom and his version of the

expectancy theory. I have to admit that, at first, I really didn't understand much of what Vroom was writing about. Even though I was an
academician myself and had published my own research studies, his
books seemed very complicated to me, and it took a long time for
Vroom's expectancy theory to sink in. But once it finally did, I felt I
had discovered something that not only was sound theoretically, but
also might have some practical value.

There were two reasons why I found Vroom's theory to be so ap-
pealing. One was that it seemed very logical; intuitively, I felt it was
true. But it also seemed a lot more comprehensive than what other
thinkers had come up with to explain the same phenomenon: what
motivates people at work. Unlike the famous trailblazers in his field—
researchers like Douglas McGregor and Frederick Herzberg—Vroom
went beyond the idea that people are motivated simply by being offered rewards or desirable outcomes. There are other factors that come
into play, Vroom said. These are the expectations that people have about
whether those outcomes can realistically be achieved and whether
they'll be truly satisfying. When it comes to motivation, in short, what
people believe is just as important as what they're offered.

Eventually, followers of Vroom refined his theory and codified the
expectations into three distinct beliefs—essential preconditions for motivation at work. The first is the belief people hold that they can perform
well enough to get what they're offered. The second is the belief that they
will actually get what they're offered. And the third is the belief that
they will find what they're offered to be satisfying to them.

Most of the popular theories of motivation concerned themselves
only with the last belief. By including the first two, the Vroom model
added greater dimension to the nature of motivation, it seemed to me,
and provided us with a more complete understanding of it. The limited interaction I had with working managers at that time also seemed
to confirm my suspicions that Vroom was on the right track. After all,
managers would tell me, how many times do we offer employees something they want, only to find out that it's not enough to motivate them
to work harder and perform better?

Intrigued by Vroom's ideas, I began to teach his expectancy theory in
my management classes and even developed seminars around him, to
see if others reacted to him in the same way that I did. To make him more
accessible to my students, I worked to simplify his language and developed some scales to measure the three beliefs. Convinced of the potential
value of Vroom's concepts, I wanted to make sure that ordinary people,
like me, could understand him and recognize the merit of his thinking.

However, it wasn't until I retired from teaching in 1980 and started
my own business that I began to think seriously about applying
Vroom's theory in a practical way. Until his ideas could be brought to a

level where managers could use them in the workplace, to my way of thinking they were virtually worthless. Without a realistic plan for management action, Vroom's model, like the other theories of motivation that preceded his, would go down in history as a brilliant mental construct, but one that did nothing to actually improve people's lives at work.

When I started to think about what I could do to bring Vroom's model to life, I focused initially on finding a connection between management and the three beliefs. And it seemed to me that Vroom was telling me this: If I wanted to have highly motivated and productive employees, I had to figure out how to manage my business in ways that would strengthen their three beliefs. So for the next six years, primarily through the process of trial and error, that's exactly what I did.

Until that time, all my knowledge of Vroom and his expectancy theory had come from books. (Those that contributed most to my understanding, and to the writing of this book, are included in the bibliography.) But once I became a manager myself, I decided to put those books aside and rely on my own judgment and experience. I developed ways to identify and diagnose problems related to motivation and performance. I experimented with various ways of managing people to find out how I could strengthen their three beliefs. And I offered training programs to teach other managers how to apply the theory.

Over time, my appreciation for Vroom's ideas grew stronger, and I became even more convinced of their validity. What impressed me most was that the theory seemed to encompass just about every kind of motivation or performance problem that arose in my company. No matter what issues we confronted that had an impact on motivation, they always seemed to relate to one or more of the three beliefs. And whenever we came up with strategies to bolster those beliefs, motivation and performance would invariably improve.

It was from that experience that I created an application model to help managers apply Vroom's theory, which I described in my first book, *Performance and Motivation Strategies for Today's Workforce* (Quorum Books, 1992). What I wanted to offer managers was a practical process that they could use to uncover and solve motivation and performance problems by evaluating and strengthening the employee beliefs related to motivation.

Since then, the application model I developed has become part of a more comprehensive approach—what I now call the belief system of motivation and performance—that many managers have used to manage change in organizations and improve motivation and performance. An important component of this system is the "one-on-one meeting," the critical interface between manager and employee that establishes the problem-solving process as a joint effort. Some of the case studies that you will read in this book occurred several years ago and involved solely the use of the application model. Others involved the more systematic approach, as in the case study of AT&T's Business Communications Services division.

This implementation gave me a wonderful opportunity to test the effectiveness of my approach on a large scale·and in an organization undergoing extensive change. It would not have been possible without the interest and confidence of my collaborator on this book, Ray Butkus. By offering his organization as a proving ground for my system, Ray provided the data and bottom-line results that help to confirm the positive impact of the belief system. And by offering his valuable time and seasoned advice, he provided me with new insights into its use and practical application.

Since then, telling managers about the belief system and developing new ways to apply it has become my life's work. And it is, perhaps, the most enjoyable and rewarding job I've ever had. For whenever managers implement this approach, they almost always derive some benefit from it. When its use is limited to a single work unit or team, it can dramatically improve interpersonal relationships and individual performance. When the belief system is applied organizationwide, the positive changes in motivation and morale that result help to propel companies to new levels of business success.

Unfortunately, despite their increased use of the belief system, most managers today still don't know who Victor Vroom is. But what these practitioners have accomplished by using the system based on his thinking is, I believe, a testament to the power of his ideas. For although Vroom is a lesser-known figure in the history of research in motivation, his work alone has successfully made the transition from theory to action. Though other thinkers in the field of industrial and organizational psychology are more widely read and recognized, it is almost impossible to determine what real impact they have had on management or how their theories have changed the work environment for the better.

After spending more than two decades of my life learning about and applying the expectancy theory, I am more certain than ever that the trail of thinking that Vroom established nearly a half century ago still provides the best course for us in dealing with the important issues related to motivation at work. My contribution has been a far less original one: to promote the practical value of Vroom's thinking and develop some simple tools that managers can use to apply it. But I hope that this utilitarian approach, which we tried to follow faithfully in this book, will make a difference in how we manage organizations and help to make our work lives more satisfying and more productive.

—**Thad B. Green**

I first became aware of the belief system approach in late 1994, when we were finalizing the development of a new sales organization at AT&T in our Business Communications Services division. We were all under a great deal of stress at that time. Not only were we attempting to build a radically new and fundamentally different organization, we were also trying to wrap up our regular, year-end activities and reach our aggressive sales goals for the year. Everyone was doing double duty.

Under such conditions, I would normally revert to the management techniques that I had been taught and relied on for years, such as the carrot-and-stick approach, to motivate my team and drive them to work harder. But given the amount of change that we were asking our people to deal with (creating the new organization involved fourteen separate change initiatives), it appeared that we had very few carrots to offer and that we'd have to wield an exceptionally big stick to accomplish our ambitious organizational goals. I became increasingly convinced that my poor motivation practices were both ineffective and emotionally draining, for both me and my subordinates. Many people in our organization were already beginning to show signs of severe strain and emotional distress, even though our transformation effort had only just begun.

It was then that a colleague of mine introduced me to Thad Green and to his approach for improving motivation and performance. Beside the results that he had achieved in previous applications, there were several things about Thad's change model that impressed me. One was the newness of it. If we were going to retool and reengineer an entirely new sales organization, I thought, then we should apply some innovative ways of motivating and managing, and the belief system was unlike anything I had ever encountered before.

I also felt that the approach could help us to understand some of the troubling emotions that were beginning to surface as a result of the transformation. Many of these appeared to be classic symptoms of change-induced trauma—irritability, explosions of temper, and the like—but they were also disturbing and disruptive and sapped people's motivation. We needed to get to their root causes, I thought, which were undoubtedly based in the fears and anxieties that were unique to each person. And it seemed to me that the belief system could help us to do that in a systematic way.

I also liked the way the belief system reinforced the notion that improving motivation and performance is a bilateral responsibility. Both managers and employees must share the burden of finding causes and solutions for problems at work and contribute equally to creating an environment that's conducive to organizational success.

There are several chapters in this book that describe how the belief system cascaded throughout our organization and that summarize the positive results we achieved. These, I hope, will show the usefulness of the approach to other organizations and help them to cope with the complex emotional issues that typically accompany change. As more and more companies transform themselves in an attempt to keep pace in a more competitive and volatile business climate, the ability of their managers to deal with the emotions triggered by change will become a major component of organizational effectiveness and, I'm convinced, a major determinant of long-term business success.

Obviously, my participation in writing this book demonstrates my strong endorsement for the belief system approach. However, there are some practical limitations to applying it which I would like to acknowledge up front. One is that it's not a "quick-fix" solution, which may disappoint those managers who continue to seek overnight remedies, even for entrenched organizational problems. Implementing the belief system effectively does require some time, and it may not produce immediate results. But when managers weigh the payback they receive against their initial investment, they usually find that the time spent has been well worthwhile—especially when their intent is to bring about lasting change.

The uniqueness of the approach may also be a limitation. Most managers are familiar with and still apply "blanket" approaches to improving motivation ("pay people more, and they will work harder"), which is regrettably the norm in business. But the underlying rationale for the belief system is exactly the opposite. It assumes that what motivates people at work is different for each and every individual. And it requires managers to get to know their employees—to "manage to the individual"—and to investigate what really works to strengthen each person's motivation.

These demands may be a drawback for some. For while most managers readily grasp the fundamental principles on which the belief system is based, more than a superficial understanding is needed to make it work. Also required is a certain sense of adventure—a desire to delve below the surface, analyze the complex problems that you find, and uncover their causes—and even some emotional risk. The belief system works best when managers aren't afraid to confront problems head on, talk about sensitive issues, and, when necessary, acknowledge their own role in causing the motivation and performance problems that they're trying to solve.

Finally, it's important to remember that the belief system is not a cure-all for anything that can go wrong in business organizations. It is not a substitute for good strategy, nor can it guarantee that the products and services you sell will bring you market success. But when it comes to improving the motivation and performance of employees, the belief system is, I'm convinced, unparalleled in its effectiveness and in its ability to bring about the change of heart and change of mind that are needed to make organizational transformations really work.

—**Raymond T. Butkus**

Acknowledgments

This book was conceived from the simple belief that large-scale organizational change can succeed only when the human dimension of change is recognized, appreciated, and managed. This belief led us on a journey of discovery and learning that continues to this day, although both of us have moved on to other work.

We are indebted to many for the final result of this work. The men and women of AT&T's Eastern Region Middle Markets provided the substance of much of the research for this book. We are grateful for their assistance, especially their patience and willingness to help us understand the power of their beliefs. Two people were especially helpful in this regard—Marianne Nosal and Jane Sanders. Their energy, zeal, enthusiasm, and commitment to excel at the change imperative chronicled in the pages that follow was a source of inspiration to us both.

We thank Michael G. Keith, Executive Vice President of AT&T, whose leadership of the national Middle Markets business provided the organizational environment where a performance culture flourished. Michael's focus on results and uncompromising commitment to excellence encouraged the managerial environment where entrepreneurship and innovation blossomed and thrived.

We also express our sincere appreciation to Clem Russo, organizer of thoughts and master of words, for his indispensable contribution.

_____ PART I

A NEW MODEL FOR MANAGING CHANGE

1

The Key to Managing
the Emotions of Change

Implementing change to become more competitive, more cost-effective, and more customer focused is the biggest challenge managers face today. To do it successfully, some will resort to extraordinary measures, as this example shows.

In a reengineering effort carried out several years ago, a critical business unit within a major financial services company underwent a massive reorganization. Traditional, functionally oriented jobs were redesigned and integrated into multiskilled service teams, middle management layers were squeezed out, and a new computer system was installed. Since virtually every employee in the division would feel the impact of these changes, serious consideration was given to ensuring high levels of involvement and motivation and to promoting the widespread acceptance of change.

Counseled by a team of outside experts, top management devised several strategies to accomplish these goals. One was to introduce a division newsletter that reported solely on the change effort. Another was to roll out the planned changes using highly participative teams. A third was to launch the change effort with great enthusiasm and fanfare. The objective here was to mount a spectacular event that everyone would remember as a turning point for the organization and the start of a bold new drive toward excellence and effectiveness.

The highlight of this affair was a talent contest that featured entertainment by several of the division's managers and supervisors. As expected, these performances were greeted with loud applause and whistles. But what elicited the greatest response from the audience was the final act of the show. That's when the division's leader—a prominent vice president within the company—appeared on stage in a clown outfit and, karaoke style, sang the lyrics to a song that was specially written for the occasion.

When this normally reserved executive was later questioned about his behavior at this event and why he risked exposing himself to public ridicule, he answered without hesitation: "I am totally committed to the success of this change effort," he said, "and I'm willing to do whatever it takes to win over the hearts and minds of my people."

THE OVERLOOKED FACTOR IN CHANGE

If you asked this executive to name the single most important factor in change, he would undoubtedly give you the same answer as most managers: people. Business books, seminars, and workshops all reinforce the same message today. Whether you're rightsizing, restructuring, reengineering, or retooling, you must focus on the people side of change. Without the support and participation of a highly motivated workforce, organizational change is simply much too difficult to carry out successfully.

Yet despite the widespread acceptance of this management precept, people problems still abound whenever organizations undertake change. Studies show conclusively, for example, that any time a restructuring is announced, turnover increases, on-the-job accidents rise, mistakes and errors multiply, and absenteeism skyrockets. No matter how well managers explain the business imperatives behind change, or how much effort they invest in formulating a new vision and communicating new corporate objectives, people react to change in negative ways and often resist it.

Even when organizations are able to effectively mobilize their people in the early stages of a change effort, it's not uncommon for people problems to surface somewhere down the road. In a recent guide to reengineering, for example, the consultants who authored the book describe a common syndrome that they call the "Terrible Twos." After an initial period of improvement that may last up to two years, they say, performance indicators in organizations that reengineer often show movement in the opposite direction: morale slumps, turnover goes up, and productivity and quality gains disappear. In some cases, these organizations actually end up worse off than they started because they lose many of the people in whose retraining they invested so much.[1]

If the managers who lead change are really focusing on their people, why does this happen? Why do people problems consistently undermine the effectiveness of change efforts? There are two possible explanations. One is that managers pay lip service to the people side of change but in reality ignore it. This may be the case in organizations where managers lack the skills or inclination to deal with difficult people problems. In these companies, managers concentrate on the aspects of change that they feel most competent to handle—namely, structural, technical, or strategic change issues—while sidestepping people problems or delegating them downward, thereby forever establishing them as a lower management priority.

Though the number of these managers may be considerable, there are also plenty of managers who *do* focus on the people side of change and still experience motivation and performance problems. What are they doing wrong? Though many of them work proactively to prevent people problems during change, what they do in most cases is insufficient to deal with the motivation and performance problems that change can cause.

Additional training, increased communication, and greater participation are a few of the standard approaches that are used to manage the people side of change. But while these strategies may be beneficial in helping people adjust to new work environments (and may even send the welcome message that managers are concerned about their people), they fail to address the one aspect of change that is consistently overlooked: how people react to change *emotionally.* And it is the emotions of change that are the key to motivation and performance whenever organizations attempt to change.

How Emotions Impact Change

Organizational change is not just about work processes, information systems, corporate structures, or business strategies. It's also about what people feel and believe: their fears and anxieties, their dreams and ambitions, their hopes and expectations. And these feelings and beliefs are so strong that they can make or break a change effort.

All too often, however, managers remain unaware of what their people really feel during organizational change. And it's not because they're bad managers. Even in the best companies, where managers are expected to demonstrate strong interpersonal skills and understand what makes their people tick, it's difficult for managers to accurately gauge the new emotional climate that change creates.

This was certainly the case in the change effort we will describe in Part IV. Though it involved the creation of a new sales organization within the Business Communications Services (BCS) division of AT&T,

many of the people who volunteered or were recruited for the startup had worked together before and were familiar to us. However, it was not until months after the change process had started, and only after lengthy interviews were conducted, that we realized the full scope and intensity of the emotions that people were feeling and how those emotions were affecting the organization's ability to change.

Why are the emotions of change so difficult to read? Part of the reason is that change makes people react in complex, unpredictable, and sometimes contradictory ways. To please their managers, for example, employees will often demonstrate enthusiasm and excitement when a change is announced—and may even feel those emotions. But what they fail to disclose are the negative feelings they experience at exactly the same time: *skepticism* about the need for change, *sadness* over the loss of established work relationships, *anger* at the way the change is handled, or *self-doubts* so severe that they interfere with the ability to work.

When one of the best account representatives in BCS later recalled his initial reaction to the change, he surprised us with this frank admission: "When they announced the change, my basic feeling was, Can I really pull this off? Even though I'm a high achiever and it looked like a great opportunity, I felt insecure and wasn't sure I could do it." In another interview conducted during the same period, a manager remembered having similar emotions: "I felt a lot of anxiety about not having enough structure in my new job," he confessed. "My greatest fear was that I wouldn't succeed, that I wouldn't reach quota, or that I'd fall to the bottom 25 percent of the pile."

The Emotional Climate of Change

• Anger	• Fear
• Anxiety	• Hope
• Confusion	• Insecurity
• Disappointment	• Sadness
• Discomfort	• Self-doubt
• Excitement	• Skepticism

Another typical response, we found, is that employees will approach a change effort with a positive mindset but then develop negative feelings as time goes on, undergoing an emotional transformation that their managers remain unaware of. A year into the BCS reorganization, for example, one sales manager made this comment during an interview: "The announcement of a new organization created a lot of excitement around here, and there was enthusiasm about starting something new. But once we got under way, things turned negative. There was anxiety among our team and a lot of stress. It was definitely not a feel-good time."

This scenario is especially common when change provides new professional opportunities but also increases responsibilities and raises expectations. For example, when the reorganization at BCS allowed one sales manager to rise to the rank of branch manager, he later remembered that he "initially felt good about the promotion and was grateful." But once the reality of his new job sank in, the principal emotions he felt were markedly different. "I began to feel that too much responsibility was placed on me too soon," he said. "I thought it was unfair. I was angry at my boss and fearful about the future, and disappointed in myself for not being able to pull it all together right away."

Even employees who embrace change may experience corollary emotions that are decidedly unpleasant—in particular, the feeling of being overwhelmed by change. A BCS account representative who was promoted to sales manager during the reorganization made this comment: "I was excited about the new challenges that the change entailed, but I felt totally overwhelmed. The time frames were tight and expectations were high, so I had a lot of adjusting to do." Said another newly promoted manager, "I was glad that I was moved up, but there was so much going on and so much that I needed to grasp that I began to develop a real fear of failing."

MANAGERS AND EMOTIONS

Why should managers be concerned about these emotions? Because the most common emotional reactions to change are those that are likely to have a negative impact on motivation and performance. Whenever change occurs at work, people experience the same emotional turmoil that they feel during major transitions in their private lives (like death, divorce, or relocation). Even when organizational change is clearly for the best, it's often perceived as a threat, and it triggers emotions that are highly personal, usually negative, and potentially disabling.

Though we came to this conclusion firsthand, there is now a small but growing number of management experts who recognize that negative emotions are pervasive during change and that they should be a primary concern of managers who lead change. In his recent book, *Mastering the Challenges of Change,* for example, former McKinsey consultant LeRoy Thompson, Jr., outlines an eight-stage sequence of emotional responses, including denial and pessimism, that he says are a "natural, normal, and necessary part of dealing with change."[2] In some cases, he suggests, giving employees "the opportunity to vent frustrations, hostilities, or fears can actually assist the change process."

Four Reactions to Change

	Typical Responses
Disengagement	• won't ask questions
	• won't seek information
	• does the minimum
Disidentification	• sulks
	• does old job
	• resists new procedures
Disorientation	• leaves work undone
	• "catastrophizes" situations
	• always asks questions
Disenchantment	• refuses to talk
	• storms out
	• yells or raises voice

A more detailed analysis of the emotions of change is presented in the book *Aftershock: Helping People Through Corporate Change*. Based on a successful seminar developed by the Wilson Learning Corporation, this book identifies four emotional stages that the authors say are typical whenever major changes are announced: disengagement, disidentification, disorientation, and disenchantment.[3] Though these emotional reactions are normal and, to a certain extent, even healthy, say the authors, they may eventually lead to damaging or dysfunctional behaviors if left unaddressed, including

- withdrawal from colleagues and friends.
- decreased initiative or lack of interest in work.
- the inability to prioritize or set goals.
- dwelling excessively on the past.
- obsessive worry.
- rumormongering, backstabbing, and sabotage.
- feelings of vulnerability, sadness, loss, anger, and resentment.

BASICS AND BENEFITS OF THE NEW CHANGE MODEL

Organizational change requires the cooperation of many people, and their motivation is critical to success. But it's not possible to maintain high levels of motivation during change without addressing the strong emotions that change stirs up. Besides implementing new structures, new strategies, and new technologies during change, managers must also focus on changing the hearts and minds of their people and on building emotional support for change.

Managing this "soft" side of change may be the hardest part of it and the area where managers most often fail. Though most managers are trained to deal with the "hard" stuff that change involves, few of them have the background, skills, or experience to manage the emotions of their people during times of change. As consultants Robert Shaw and A. Elise Walton state in the book *Discontinuous Change,* "Changing the soft part of organizational life requires a different set of change management techniques and greater sophistication on the part of change agents."[4]

What makes this task even more difficult is that managers can seldom depend on their organizations to help them out. In most companies there are no effective channels that employees and managers can use to communicate and discuss emotions. Existing mechanisms—like performance evaluations or staff meetings—are unsuitable settings for such discussions and don't create a comfortable environment in which emotions can be expressed openly and honestly.

This is not to say that organizations in change don't worry about motivation or attempt to improve it. Most of them do, though they usually rely on the same motivation strategies that businesses have been using for years, such as pep talks, warnings, pats on the back, and incentive programs. Based on the carrot-and-stick approach to people management, these strategies all share the same implicit assumption: If you offer employees rewards for performing well (like praise, bonuses, or promotions), or make it clear what will happen if they *don't* perform, then motivation will automatically increase and managers will get the results they want.

Unfortunately, these strategies have an uneven track record for improving motivation and may be especially ineffective during times of change. How often, for example, do companies implement new and expensive incentive programs that fail to have a substantial impact on employee performance? And what good does it do to offer promotions and raises if your company is undergoing the kinds of changes (like downsizing) that reduce the likelihood that you can deliver on those promises?

Perhaps the biggest drawback of incentive programs is that they don't address the emotions of change, and there are two specific reasons why. One is that they assume motivation is a purely rational decision, so they tend to ignore the emotions completely. The other is that they assume everyone is motivated by the *same* rewards or punishments, so they apply a blanket approach to motivation. Since both assumptions are wrong, incentive programs have little to offer in managing the emotions of change and cannot respond to the diverse emotional needs that employees demonstrate during change.

However, one new approach to improving motivation has been able to do this effectively and with proven results. This approach is called the belief system of motivation and performance.[5] It has been implemented in dozens of corporations, including Delta Air Lines, Lucent Technologies, Metropolitan Life Insurance Company, and Holiday Inn. In this book we'll describe how it's been applied effectively with individuals, teams, and organizations and show how it works during large-scale change.

This approach is based on the idea that what employees *feel and believe* is far more important than what they're *offered* by managers to motivate them. As a result, it works better than incentive programs to improve motivation because it focuses on what people feel during change, provides a structured process that allows their emotions to surface, and helps to overcome the emotional barriers to change.

The Model in Brief

Like traditional incentive programs, the belief system recognizes that employees must be offered things they want in order to be motivated and to perform. But merely offering rewards isn't enough. If it were, incentive programs would work perfectly (and we know they don't), and improving motivation would be easy (and we know it isn't). What else is needed? With this new approach, managers don't rely solely on external rewards to improve motivation. Since motivation is an internal process unique to individuals, managers utilize a more personalized strategy for improving motivation and focus on what each employee truly feels and believes.

There are three specific beliefs that managers focus on:

Belief-1 (B-1): Can I do it? Unless employees believe that they can, in fact, do what they are being asked to do, they won't be motivated.

Belief-2 (B-2): Will outcomes be tied to my performance? Unless employees believe that they will really get the outcomes they are offered when they perform as expected, they won't be motivated.

Belief-3 (B-3): Will outcomes be satisfying to me? Unless employees believe that the rewards they're promised are things they truly want, they won't be motivated.

Though managers often assume that employees hold these beliefs to be true, in many change situations employees really don't. And unless all three are firmly "believed" by employees, it is unlikely that they will be motivated to change (no matter how attractive the rewards offered), and they may experience many of the negative emotions associated with change.

Conditions for Motivation

B-1: "I can do it."

B-2: "Outcomes will be tied to my performance."

B-3: "Outcomes will be satisfying to me."

Consider Belief-1, for example. If a reengineering effort increases workloads and adds new responsibilities, employees may feel unqualified for their jobs or think they lack the skills to perform them well. In this situation, some will conclude that they're unable to reach their performance expectations ("I just can't do it"), and may develop feelings of anxiety or frustration.

Belief-2 is also frequently undermined during change efforts, because that's when the link between performance and outcomes often weakens. When popular managers are terminated as a result of downsizing, for example, or when some of the best people are sacrificed to cut costs, many employees start to doubt the connection between performance and outcomes, become skeptical and distrustful of their organization, and lose their motivation.

Change efforts may also negatively affect Belief-3. This is because organizations in change cannot always give employees what they may want most, like raises, promotions, or job security. In some cases, in fact, the best performers receive rewards that many would consider undesirable, such as increased accountability or a bigger span of control. The result is that employees become angry, resentful, and sometimes rebellious, and their motivation takes a turn for the worse.

How does the belief system help? It provides a structured and easy-to-use process managers can apply to (1) diagnose any motivation and performance problems associated with change, and (2) come up with solutions to those problems that are acceptable to both managers and their direct reports. This approach is especially effective for handling motivation and performance problems related to change because

- It provides a comfortable setting—the one-on-one session—where managers and employees can discuss sensitive and emotionally charged issues.
- It uncovers the specific motivation issues that lie behind the emotions of change, and it encourages managers and their people to work together to resolve them.

- It identifies motivation problems in the early stages—before they get out of hand and impede change—and it provides an ongoing system for follow-up and review.

The Motivation Payoff

There are three characteristics of this approach that explain its strong appeal to managers:

1. *It is a system.* The belief system is a comprehensive approach to improving motivation that can help managers address the motivation problems associated with change.
2. *It focuses on the individual.* The belief system relieves managers of the burden of improving motivation on their own. It recognizes that employees know more about their motivation problems than anyone else, and it involves them as partners in solving those problems.
3. *It promotes effective communication.* The belief system improves working relationships between managers and their direct reports by helping them develop a more informed understanding of each other.

Another important reason why managers appreciate this approach is that it helps to improve *their* motivation. Remember, managers themselves often feel frustrated, insecure, or confused during change, because in many cases they have to confront people problems they never encountered before and cope with a wide range of disruptive emotions without the proper support or tools. In addition, some managers are not convinced that spending time to manage emotions is worthwhile or that it necessarily results in a smoother change process. Is it any wonder, then, that management motivation flags during change, or that some managers become less accessible to their people than they were before?

Using the belief system approach, however, managers often develop a renewed sense of self-confidence, and many say they become better managers in general. Not only does this approach help them tap into what their people feel, it also creates a safe environment for motivation problems to surface and be dealt with. Finally, it provides the proof managers need of what can be gained by managing the emotions of change.

In short, this approach helps managers meet the three conditions that are required for improved motivation:

Belief-1: I can do it. Managers acquire an effective tool for managing the emotions of change.

Belief-2: Outcomes will be tied to my performance. Managers understand how much more effective they can be when they work to manage the emotions of change.

Belief-3: Outcomes will be satisfying to me. Managers who lead change achieve more desirable results: a smoother change process and greater success at mobilizing their people to implement change.

CASE STUDY PREVIEW

In the following chapters, we'll present a variety of applications of the belief system approach and two case studies that involve organizational change. Using the results of internal surveys, we'll include data to show the impact of the approach on these organizations over time, demonstrate how it improved employee morale and motivation, and explain how it worked at different organizational levels.

The longer case study involves BCS, one of the twenty-three units that made up AT&T before its "trivestiture" in 1996, and now a $20-billion business that provides telecommunications solutions to companies of all sizes. In this example, we'll focus on the sales organization within BCS and, more specifically, on the Eastern Region of what is called Middle Markets, a new sales entity that was launched in 1995. A sizable organization in its own right, the Eastern Region of Middle Markets covers thirteen states and the District of Columbia, accounts for one-third of all Middle Markets customers and revenues, and employs over 800 people, including account representatives, sales managers, and support staff.

Middle Markets was created to target mid-size business users, a segment of customers that BCS had historically neglected but which came to represent a huge and relatively unexplored opportunity in the 1990s—some 45 thousand businesses in all! Though BCS already serviced some mid-size companies, the vast majority of its accounts were either large corporate customers or relatively small, family-owned enterprises.

Starting a new sales organization from scratch was a huge undertaking, even for a well-established business like BCS, and there was no guarantee of success. Despite its membership in a prestigious corporate family, BCS faced stiff competition for mid-size customers in all its markets and was not set up to find, sell to, or service those customers adequately. To effectively penetrate this market, BCS had to implement major changes in the way prospects were qualified, in the skills salespeople applied when selling, in the strategies used to develop customer relationships, and in the support systems the organization relied on. The bottom line was that BCS had to develop an entirely new sales model and create a totally different sales culture.

This presented an exciting opportunity for the people who joined Middle Markets, but it was also a difficult, draining, and sometimes traumatic experience. Needless to say, everything possible was done to ensure success. A new organizational structure was designed, extensive training was carried out, a customized compensation system was installed, and careful steps were taken to provide salespeople with the tools they needed to sell differently. Yet despite all these efforts to manage change and to moderate the fallout from it, change was to take an emotional toll on the organization that was not anticipated or planned for.

What the belief system did for Middle Markets was to help its people in the Eastern Region work through the emotions of change so they did not become an obstacle to change. This required considerable work on the part of both managers and employees, and its impact was not felt overnight. But it did make a difference, so much so that the approach has now become an integral part of the organization's culture.

Why does it work? As one BCS manager put it, "The belief system works because it's so elegantly simple. It affects your most important relationships at work and doesn't stop at the intellectual level. It gets to your emotions, and pulls you into what you're really all about." And for the minimal amount of time and energy you need to invest in the process, the payback can be significant. "In retrospect, I have to say that the belief system is the most profound developmental experience I've had in my 23 years at AT&T," another manager recently told us. "For the few hours invested, the output is tremendous."

In the pages that follow, we'll describe this approach more thoroughly and show how it can help organizations do a better job of implementing and managing change.

NOTES

1. Robert Janson, Dennis Attenello, and John Uzzi, *Reengineering for Results: A Step-by-Step Guide* (New York: Quality Resources, 1995), 171.

2. LeRoy Thompson, Jr., *Mastering the Challenges of Change: Strategies for Each Stage in Your Organization's Life Cycle* (New York: AMACOM, 1994), 158.

3. Harry Woodward and Steve Buchholz, *Aftershock: Helping People Through Corporate Change* (New York: John Wiley & Sons, 1987), 92–115. The emotional reactions described in this book were originally described by psychologist William Bridges in *Transitions: Making Sense of Life's Changes* (Reading, Mass.: Addison-Wesley, 1980).

4. David Nadler, Robert B. Shaw, A. Elise Walton, and Associates, *Discontinuous Change: Leading Organizational Transformation* (San Francisco: Jossey-Bass, 1995), 275.

5. Previously published works on the belief system of motivation and performance include Thad Green, *Performance and Motivation Strategies for Today's Workforce: A Guide to Expectancy Theory Applications* (Westport, Conn.: Quorum Books, 1992); Thad Green and Merwyn Hayes, *The Belief System: The Secret to Motivation and Improved Performance* (Winston-Salem, N.C.: Beechwood Press, 1993); and Thad Green and Bill Barkley, *Manage to the Individual—If You Want to Know, Ask!: A Story about the Belief System of Motivation and Performance* (Atlanta, Ga.: The Belief System Institute, 1995).

2

Solving Motivation and Performance Problems

It was a major turning point in the development of human civilization some five thousand years ago when cattle were domesticated for draft purposes. For the first time since the dawn of agriculture, nearly seven thousand years earlier, something other than human muscle could be applied to tilling the land. The yoke was the instrument that made this breakthrough possible. A simple device fashioned from wood, it fit painlessly over the ox's head and neck and allowed farmers to effectively transfer the power of that animal to plow.

Yet another thousand years would pass before horses were domesticated. Why the delay? When horses were first yoked to plows, they invariably choked themselves to death. A second innovation was required—the horse collar—to harness the superior power of the horse for farming. Though the yoke worked well with oxen, it was not appropriate for the horse, an animal with a very different muscular and skeletal structure.

There is an important lesson to be learned from this story of our early ancestors: Just as the yoke was ineffective—even harmful—when applied to the horse, so too are some of the tools that managers still use to maximize performance at work. Far too many managers apply techniques of motivation that are outdated, counterproductive, and ill-suited to the employees they manage today.[1]

To be sure, employees are not animals to be yoked or collared. But the analogy leads us to wonder how far the traditional carrot-and-stick approach to motivation has really taken us. And why do so many managers still use the simple and unsophisticated techniques that derive from it? Though we may never know the answer to the first question, the answer to the second one is fairly obvious: Most managers feel they have no alternative.

Newer approaches to motivation have been developed, of course. In the past half century, a number of prominent thinkers—including Abraham Maslow, Frederick Herzberg, and Douglas McGregor—have outlined theories to explain what *really* motivates people at work and what managers must do to improve performance. But most of these theories don't translate well into the realities of the workplace, and they come with no practical guidelines for utilization. As a result, many managers fall back on the same strategies that their bosses used to motivate them: above all, incentive programs.

The Way Incentives Work

All incentive programs are based on a formula for improving motivation that involves four basic variables: effort, performance, outcomes, and satisfaction. The logic behind these programs goes something like this: Employees will put in the right amount of *effort* to meet *performance* expectations if they receive the kinds of *outcomes* (raises, promotions, etc.) that will give them *satisfaction*. In short, offer your people what they want, and they'll work hard to get it (or offer them what they don't want, and they'll work hard to avoid it).

Effort → Performance → Outcomes → Satisfaction

As we saw in Chapter 1, however, the problem with most incentive programs is that they focus solely on the offering of outcomes and ignore the three beliefs that are the key to making the motivation formula work:

B-1: "Can I do it?"
B-2: "Will outcomes be tied to my performance?"
B-3: "Will outcomes be satisfying to me?"

The first belief deals with the relationship between employee effort and performance. The second deals with the relationship between performance and outcomes. And the third deals with the relationship between outcomes and satisfaction. These three beliefs form the foundation of the belief system of motivation and performance.

B-1   B-2   B-3
Effort → Performance → Outcomes → Satisfaction

Understanding that these beliefs are critical preconditions for motivation helps to explain why incentive programs generally yield such lackluster results. Because employees don't always hold these beliefs to be true, attempts to improve motivation by using incentives can fail, even when the incentives are highly desirable ones!

Types of Motivation Problems

B-1: "I can't do it."

Motivation problem:	lack of *confidence*
Associated feelings:	self-doubt
	anxiety
	frustration

B-2: "Outcomes are not tied to my performance."

Motivation problem:	lack of *trust*
Associated feelings:	skepticism
	disbelief
	mistrust

B-3: "Outcomes will not be satisfying to me."

Motivation problem:	lack of *satisfaction*
Associated feelings:	anger
	rebelliousness
	resentment

A major change effort only complicates the situation. If B-1, B-2, or B-3 beliefs are shaky to begin with, organizational change can weaken them even further. The result is often serious motivation and performance problems—at a time when organizations can least afford them—and a corresponding surge in the negative emotions associated with change.

When an employee believes "I can't do it," for example, he or she may develop a lack of self-confidence and begin to experience many of the unpleasant feelings that go along with it: self-doubt, anxiety, frustration. About a year into the change effort at BCS, one manager described the inner turmoil he went through by comparing the restructuring to "building a ship at the same time you're trying to sail it.

I was very concerned about how this could be done," he said, "and at the time I felt completely frustrated."

Employee beliefs that "outcomes are not tied to my performance" can also lead to significant motivation problems, especially lack of trust. This is normally accompanied by feelings of skepticism or disbelief, precisely the emotions that another manager felt when he was told early on in the BCS change effort that power would be allocated differently. "No matter what they told me, I didn't believe it," he said. "So I just kept waiting for somebody to give me orders. With every change effort in the past, we were told we would be empowered, but we weren't."

Employee beliefs that "outcomes will not be satisfying to me" often lead to a third major problem, chronic dissatisfaction, and to feelings of anger, rebelliousness, and resentment. A case in point: When sales representatives at BCS first joined the new Middle Markets organization, some felt a loss of prestige in giving up the big-name national accounts they had been working on. "A few of my reps became so angry that they just walked out on me," a manager revealed. "There were such strong feelings of rejection that we were constantly witnessing irrational and emotional outbursts."

UNCOVERING MOTIVATION PROBLEMS

Just as the negative emotions associated with change can often go undetected and unaddressed, the motivation and performance problems that cause them frequently remain hidden and unresolved. Because of this, managers who lead change are sometimes frustrated in their efforts. They fail to realize that it's not enough to appeal to the intellect of their employees. They must also win over their hearts in order to implement change successfully.

Why are motivation problems so difficult to uncover? Part of the reason is that employees are afraid to speak about them or even admit that they exist. Though most employees know when they have a motivation problem, many feel that acknowledging it is tantamount to admitting failure, and, naturally, they don't want to appear weak or incompetent to their manager.

These fears and inhibitions intensify during times of change, and it's not hard to understand why. Whenever organizations attempt to change, their employees begin to worry: about losing their status, losing their reputation, or even losing their jobs. A change that involves work redesign or new technologies, for example, can easily trigger feelings of insecurity or inadequacy. When the change involves layoffs (as many restructurings do), employees become even more defensive. Instead of talking openly about their motivation problems, they are more likely to do just the opposite. They clam up, stifle their fears, and try to project an attitude of competence and self-confidence.

No matter how threatening a change may appear, however, most employees would be willing to discuss their fears and problems if their manager initiated the discussion. But managers rarely do. Many of them become so involved in the strategic or tactical aspects of change that they fail to notice what's going on with their people or tune out the emotional signals that point to major problems. In many cases, it's only when these problems reach a critical stage—when large numbers of employees begin to jump ship, or when quality and productivity deteriorate—that managers even realize anything is wrong. By that time, they can only guess at what caused the problems and what solutions might be effective in turning the situation around.

Getting to the Source

The belief system approach is a practical method that can help managers resolve these problems during change effectively. It takes the guesswork out of the search for motivation problems and alerts managers to the three principal types:

- motivation problems caused by a lack of confidence.
- motivation problems caused by a lack of trust.
- motivation problems caused by a lack of satisfaction.

The approach is based on the expectancy theory of motivation and on the research of Yale University professor Victor H. Vroom. In conducting his analyses of why motivation improvement so often fails, Vroom came to the conclusion that motivation at work depends on certain employee expectations or beliefs: that effort will lead to performance, that performance will lead to outcomes, and that these outcomes, when received, will be satisfying.

Like other expectancy theorists, Vroom maintained that the tendency of people to act in certain ways depends on the strength of the expectation that their actions will be followed by certain outcomes and on the perceived value—or "valence"—of those outcomes. This combination of expectation and valence is what determines people's behavior, Vroom and his colleagues argued, and unless both expectation and valence are present to some degree, there will be little or no motivation to act. For example, if a person wants a certain outcome but doesn't feel it can be achieved through his or her efforts, then that person won't be motivated. Similarly, that person will also lack motivation if he or she believes that a certain outcome *can* be achieved but is undesirable.

What distinguished Vroom from other expectancy theorists was his attempt to use the theory to analyze motivation in the workplace. And the research he conducted, outlined in his now classic 1964 book, *Work and Motivation,* led to his breakthrough thinking about beliefs— that in order to understand motivation at work, we must consider people's beliefs about the likelihood that they can perform and their beliefs about whether their performance will lead to outcomes that they want.[2]

In the decades that followed the publication of Vroom's theories, most behavioral scientists agreed that his analysis of motivation was comprehensive and valid. But no one could figure out how to apply it directly within the work environment until one of the authors of this book, Thad Green, developed the belief system model. Through this model, Vroom's original application of the expectancy theory was transformed into a practical tool that managers can use to improve motivation and performance at work.

How does the belief system approach actually work? The application model that Green developed relies on structured, facilitated meetings between managers and their direct reports to find the answers to the three basic questions that uncover motivation problems:

- *Does the employee believe that his or her effort will lead to the expected performance* (B-1)?
- *Does the employee believe that outcomes will be tied to his or her performance* (B-2)?
- *Does the employee believe the outcomes will be satisfying* (B-3)?

Preconditions for Employee Motivation

An employee is motivated to perform when

1. The employee believes that effort will lead to performance (B-1).
2. The employee believes that performance will lead to outcomes (B-2).
3. The employee believes that outcomes will lead to satisfaction (B-3).

Once a manager has identified a specific motivation problem, he or she can then work with the employee to find its cause and develop an appropriate solution. Though the critical event in this approach is the initial one-on-one session for managers and employees, the belief system model can be implemented as a continuous process that involves regular follow-up sessions about every six months. These sessions reinforce agreed-upon solutions and work to sustain the new levels of communication that help avert potential or recurring motivation and performance problems.

This model works remarkably well—far better than managers expect—and there are several reasons why:

- It prepares managers and employees for solving motivation problems by getting them to think about these issues *before* they meet. "Preparing for the one-on-one discussion caused me to think about a lot of things that I was wrestling with," said one manager who applied the approach.

- It promotes effective change by clarifying expectations, uncovering hidden agendas, and managing emotions before they escalate. "The belief system has helped me to try to understand and solve a problem situation, instead of just reacting emotionally to it," said another manager.

- It relies on the cooperation and involvement of the one person who knows most about the problem and what may be causing it: the employee. "I use the belief system now to analyze every problem I have that deals with people," another manager said.

By gently forcing an accurate diagnosis of problems and their causes, the belief system model increases the prospects of finding good solutions to performance shortfalls. After all, it takes information to solve problems, and the goal of the belief system model is to uncover critical information about performance and motivation and to guide managers and employees in applying it productively.

In doing so, the model works to create an environment in which managers and employees share the responsibility for solving performance problems, and it fosters the kind of communication that helps managers maintain the critical preconditions for employee motivation: confidence in their ability to meet performance expectations, trust in others to tie outcomes to performance, and satisfaction with their job and the outcomes that they receive.

Using a Structured Approach

If there's one principle that guides this entire approach, it's the idea that managers can best identify and solve change-related motivation and performance problems by going directly to their source. If you want to know what's wrong, in other words, ask the person who's experiencing the problem.

If you suspect that an employee has a motivation or performance problem related to Belief-1, for example, you can uncover the problem by asking questions like these:

- "Do you know what's expected of you?"
- "Do you think that what's expected of you is attainable?"
- "Can you do what you're being asked to do?"
- "Do you see any problems in doing what you're being asked to do?"

To find out if an employee has a problem related to Belief-2, you should ask questions like these:

- "What do you expect to get if you do a good job?"
- "What do you expect to get if you perform poorly?"
- "Do people who do a good job around here get what they deserve?"
- "In your opinion, have we come through on our promises in the past?"

To find out if an employee has a problem related to Belief-3, you might ask these questions:

- "Do you want all the things being offered to you?"
- "Is there anything that you're not getting that you want?"
- "Is there anything that you're getting that you don't want?"
- "Are you getting the challenge, recognition, feedback, and enjoyment that you want from your job?"

Managers can formulate and ask questions like these on their own, or they can devise a structured, written questionnaire (like the one described in Chapter 7 and used in the implementation described in Chapter 8), that they and their direct reports can fill out before their one-on-one session. Having such a questionnaire requires both parties to think long and hard about potential B-1, B-2, and B-3 problems before they meet. Then, when they sit down together to talk, they can compare their responses, clarify the issues to be resolved, and develop a written action plan.

To get to the bottom of deep-seated B-1 problems, for example, the questionnaire might ask managers and employees to make a list of the most important parts of the employee's job and then indicate the degree of effort given to each task and the performance level normally achieved. To uncover B-2 problems, the questionnaire might ask both parties to indicate how much they agree or disagree with a series of statements (e.g., "Promotions are based on performance" or "People usually get what they deserve here"). A third component of the questionnaire should focus on B-3 problems and seek to determine if employees are not getting enough of the outcomes they want or are getting too many outcomes they don't want.

Some managers have also implemented the approach using a worksheet that identifies a specific motivation and performance problem before the one-on-one session takes place (not reaching revenue goals, for example). This allows the manager and employee to separately analyze why the problem is occurring and how it can be solved, and then compare their responses in their one-on-one session.

Whether or not managers use worksheets like these, however, the effectiveness of the approach is always enhanced when both parties fully understand the intent of the belief system model. When they know beforehand how it's used and why it's in their best interest to participate, they're almost always more willing to share the responsibility of solving motivation and performance problems and usually work harder to do so.

Many managers have also found it valuable to have a trained facilitator present during each one-on-one session. The reason is that an unbiased third party who's familiar with the belief system approach can help keep the session focused and on schedule, and provide assistance in navigating through the difficult and often emotional issues that arise.

FINDING CAUSES AND SOLUTIONS

The belief system works because it gives managers the opportunity to find out what their people really feel and believe. In the context of this approach, employee comments that previously might have been viewed as signs of a bad attitude, resistance, or troublemaking instead become valuable bits of information that can be used to diagnose problems. "The belief system has helped us become a more reflective group," one BCS manager recently said. "We're more aware of ourselves and the impact we have on each other, and we understand better why we act the way we do."

Another advantage of this approach is that it allows managers to actually measure motivation levels and to isolate problem areas more easily by logging employee responses into simple rating scales. To determine if a B-1 problem exists and how severe it is, for example, a manager can construct a scale with a range, say, of 0 to 10, with 0 representing the lowest level of employee confidence ("I cannot perform as expected") and 10 representing the highest level ("I can perform as expected").

With minor variations, similar scales can be constructed for B-2 and B-3 responses. Absolute precision in interpreting what employees say

and in logging their responses is not critical here; thoughtful "guessti-
mates" will work fine. What is important, however, is that managers
ask questions that pertain to each one of the three beliefs, and that
they ask enough questions to gather all the information needed to recognize a problem.

Interpreting B-1 Responses

0	1	2	3	4	5	6	7	8	9	10

I cannot perform   *Not sure.*   *I can perform*
    as expected.   *as expected.*

"I can't do it."   "I'm not sure   "I can do it."
                    I can do it."

"It's impossible."   "Maybe I can."   "I know exactly
                              what's expected
                              of me."

"I don't know how."   "I might be able to." "No sweat."

"I don't know what's   "I'm not sure what's "I have no problems
   expected."   expected of me."   with that."

Interpreting B-2 Responses

1	2	3	4	5	6	7	8	9	10

Outcomes are not   *Not sure.*   *Outcomes are*
    tied to my   *tied to my*
    performance.   *performance.*

"What you get is not   "There's a 50–50   "If you perform
   based on how well   chance."   well, they take
   you perform."   care of you."

"You never get what   "May get it, or may   "You always get
   what you deserve   not. You never   what you
   here."   know."   deserve here."

"Outcomes are   "Wouldn't be   "Outcomes are
   never tied to   surprised either   always tied
   performance."   way."   to performance."

Responses that fall in the top third of each scale usually indicate
that no motivation problem exists. Responses that fall in the middle
third suggest potential motivation problems. And responses that fall
in the lower third point to serious problems.

Interpreting B-3 Responses

−10	−8	−6	−4	−2	0	+2	+4	+6	+8	+10

Outcomes   *Outcomes slightly*   *Outcomes slightly*   *Outcomes*
dissatisfying   *dissatisfying*   *satisfying*   *satisfying*

"I would hate that."   *"I can take it*   *"I would love it."*
                     or leave it."

"Couldn't live with that."   *"Either way is fine*   *"I'd kill for it."*
                           with me."

                       "It doesn't matter to   *"I want it more*
                       me one way or   *than anything."*
                       the other."

Probing for Underlying Causes

Once a problem has been identified and appears to be significant, the next step is to uncover the causes of the problem and to find an appropriate solution for it. Though many managers attempt to solve motivation and performance problems without first identifying their cause, this hit-or-miss approach usually relies on generic solutions that ignore the specific issues at hand and sometimes create more problems than they solve.

To find out the real cause of a motivation or performance problem, it's necessary to go directly to the source. In most cases, simply by asking questions of the employee who's experiencing the problem, managers can find out not only that a problem exists, but also the important issues surrounding the problem and the major factors contributing to it.

No special interviewing expertise is required to uncover this information. Any manager can do it simply by asking open, neutral, and probing questions. Here are some examples of the types of questions that should be asked:

- Why do you feel that way?
- Can you tell me more about that?
- What's behind your thinking on this?
- What happened to make you feel this way?
- Can you tell me more about what's going on?
- Can you be more specific?

What managers find out by asking questions like these will depend on which of the three types of motivation problems the employee is experiencing:

Confidence Problems (B-1)

Employees typically experience a lack of confidence when (1) they don't have the adequate skills to perform their job, (2) they harbor unrealistic expectations about their job, or (3) they don't have enough resources or authority to get their job done. Employees are particularly vulnerable to this problem during times of change, because that's when they are often asked to perform new jobs or take on different responsibilities.

Trust Problems (B-2)

Employees typically experience a lack of trust when (1) their organization lacks systems that reward people for performance, (2) they define "performance" or "results" differently from their managers, or (3) they have a history of not getting what they deserve. Employees are especially vulnerable to this problem during times of change because organizations in transition sometimes base staffing decisions on factors other than performance (cost of labor, for example).

Satisfaction Problems (B-3)

Employees typically experience a lack of satisfaction when (1) they don't receive the outcomes they want, (2) they receive outcomes they don't want (like more work), or (3) they don't find their work rewarding enough. Employees are particularly vulnerable to this problem during times of change, because the number and types of rewards that organizations in transition can offer are frequently limited or curtailed.

Identifying Effective Solutions

Some of the motivation and performance problems that are caused by change call for obvious solutions. If an employee feels frustrated because she doesn't have the right technical skills for her new job, sending her to a computer course at a local college may eliminate the problem completely. If an employee is dissatisfied with his job because his workload has suddenly increased, hiring additional help (when budgets permit) or eliminating certain requirements may provide an easy solution.

In many change situations, however, the most effective way to resolve a problem isn't always self-evident. That's because motivation and performance problems are often unique to individuals and therefore require specific and sometimes customized solutions. Consequently, managers should always involve employees in finding

---

Motivation and Performance Problems: Typical Causes and Solutions

---

Motivation Problem	Typical Causes	Solution Approaches
Confidence (B-1)	Inadequate skills.	Provide training or coaching.
	Unrealistic expectations.	Establish realistic expectations.
	Not enough resources or authority.	Increase resources and authority for the position.
Trust (B-2)	Outcomes not tied to performance.	Tie outcomes to performance.
	Employee and manager define performance differently.	Clarify performance expectations.
	History of outcomes not being tied to performance.	Consistently offer outcomes based on performance.
Satisfaction (B-3)	Not receiving desired outcomes.	Offer desired outcomes, when possible.
	Receiving unwanted outcomes.	Withhold unwanted outcomes.
	Work not rewarding.	Redesign job or transfer employee.

---

solutions to their motivation problems (no matter how obvious the solution may at first appear) by asking questions like, "What do you think we should do here?" or "How do you think we should handle this?" There are three important reasons why:

1. *Employees are the best source for solutions.* Since employees live with their motivation and performance problems daily, they usually know what caused them and how to fix them.
2. *Employee solutions are usually better.* Solutions suggested by employees tend to be less complicated, less costly, and more effective than those their managers recommend.
3. *Employees want to be involved in finding solutions.* Employees are eager to help solve their own problems; in most cases, all they need is the opportunity and the encouragement.

This is not to say that every motivation and performance problem can be solved quickly and easily. Some solutions that employees propose—or that may readily resolve a motivation problem—may not be available to managers, especially during times of change. For example, an employee believes that getting a promotion would improve his motivation, but the company is in a downsizing mode; an employee says she requires more money in order to be motivated, but payroll budgets have been slashed to cut costs; or a supervisor is requesting additional help, but the organization has imposed a hiring freeze.

What can managers do when the solutions to problems are not apparent or available? There are four steps in the belief system approach that managers can follow to resolve especially difficult motivation problems:

1. *Level with the employee.* Be open and honest; if you can't give employees what they want, say so and explain why: "I know that you're interested in moving up in the company, but we've eliminated so many management positions that no promotion opportunities are available now."

2. *Give the problem to the employee to solve.* Let employees know that they share the responsibility in solving their problems: "I know that you want a raise, but there's just no money for that right now and my hands are tied. Is there anything you can suggest that would help us resolve this dilemma?"

3. *Offer substitutions or offsets.* Try to compensate for the desired outcomes that employees are not getting by probing to uncover attractive substitutes that are within your control: "With this merger going on, it clearly won't be possible for you to hire anyone new in your department. Let's explore some possibilities that might get you over the disappointment of not getting extra help." Another effective strategy is to offset the dissatisfaction that comes with an undesired outcome by offering additional outcomes than can outweigh the negatives: "I know you're not looking forward to all the traveling you'll have to do in your new sales job, but how would you feel if we gave you a company car for your trips that you could also use in your personal time?"

4. *When all else fails, "level bold."* As a last resort, let employees know that if they cannot come up with a workable solution—and will not accept substitutions or offsets—you really have only one choice: "It appears that you have a problem we can't resolve, and this is not something I can live with. Though you have many excellent capabilities, your performance here is unacceptable. So I suggest that you start thinking about other opportunities that might suit you better—either elsewhere within this company or within another organization."

Even in situations like these, where the only solution is a clearly unpleasant one, managers who use the belief system often report improved employee relations. Why does this happen? Because the process itself demonstrates respect and concern for employees, and they respond to that in a positive way. "At least my manager was willing to listen to me," employees will say after their one-on-one session, or, "The fact that she went the whole nine yards to solve my problem shows that she really cares."

Simply by trying to find acceptable solutions to motivation and performance problems, and by involving employees in the effort, managers who apply this approach usually end up with significantly higher levels of employee satisfaction and performance.

A CHANGE TOOL WITH UNIVERSAL APPLICATION

While the focus of this book is the use of the belief system in managing organizational change, its application is far broader. Motivation and performance problems are certainly not exclusive to organizations in transition. Unfortunately, these problems are pervasive in our times and all managers can expect to see an increase in both their frequency and severity.

For those managers who lead change, however, the approach we're describing is an especially powerful tool because it helps them to deal more effectively with the emotions of change and to solve the motivation and performance problems that lie beneath those emotions. In addition, it can help those managers create an organizational climate more conducive to change and enhance their ability to implement change successfully. There are five specific ways it does this:

1. *By improving communication during change.* Though many managers increase written communications and hold more meetings during change, they often overlook the one form of communication the belief system approach relies on most: interpersonal communication.

2. *By promoting better understanding during change.* During a time when misunderstandings between managers and their direct reports are more likely to occur, the belief system works to correct preconceived notions, remove biases, and eliminate misperceptions.

3. *By ensuring that everyone's goals are aligned during change.* By helping managers to better understand what their employees want, and by helping employees to better understand what their managers need, the belief system works to identify individual and organizational priorities and promotes greater alignment within organizations.

4. *By improving employee motivation to change.* By helping employees to get the outcomes they want, the belief system increases their job satisfaction during change, as well as their willingness to change.

5. *By improving management motivation to lead change.* By providing tools for managers to deal with the emotions of change and the motivation problems associated with them, the belief system helps managers achieve better results during change and enhances their confidence and ability to lead change.

In Part II we will provide real-life examples of how the belief system has been applied with individuals, with teams, and with entire organizations.

NOTES

1. This story of oxen and the yoke is recounted by quality expert W. Edwards Deming in *Out of the Crisis* (Cambridge: MIT Center for Advanced Engineering Study, 1986).

2. For more information, see Victor H. Vroom, *Work and Motivation* (New York: John Wiley & Sons, 1964).

_____ PART II

APPLYING THE
CHANGE MODEL WITH
INDIVIDUALS, TEAMS, AND
ORGANIZATIONS

3

Leading Individuals to Change

Robert M. had always been in sales—at least throughout his adult life—and was convinced that he could sell anything to anybody. But in his late forties he accepted a position in a new company and, for the first time, he began to question his professional abilities. In all his previous jobs, Robert could rely on his personal charm and strong people skills to ensure a successful sale. Now, selling highly technical products to business customers, he had to demonstrate a completely different set of sales competencies: strong product knowledge, in-depth understanding of customer needs, and the ability to maintain long-term business relationships. During the first few months in his new job, Robert was determined to succeed, and he worked hard. But then one day he gave in to his frustration and said to himself, "I just can't do it anymore." At this point, he lost his motivation and quit trying, and he began to search for a position elsewhere.

The emotions that Robert felt throughout this experience were similar to those that many people feel when faced with major changes at work: first excitement, then apprehension mixed with anxiety, then fear, and finally frustration and hopelessness. And like many others who find themselves in a change-related work situation, Robert tried to hide his negative emotions and project an attitude of confidence.

But the attempts to conceal his true feelings didn't always work. He often appeared edgy and nervous in the office and was sometimes rude to customers on sales calls.

Robert's boss did not spend much time thinking about his employees' feelings or trying to interpret what they meant. But he was concerned about performance, and Robert's was not up to par. After months on the job, the seasoned sales professional he thought his company had hired was still far short of meeting his quota, and there were worrisome calls coming in from some of Robert's customers.

What eventually happened to Robert? In a moment of despair, he could have quit his job. Or his boss, disappointed in Robert's performance, could have asked him to leave. But Robert actually stayed on in that sales position and, in time, regained his status as a top performer. Today, he's an executive in the same company he was planning to leave and is a widely recognized expert in conducting sales of high technology.

The belief system of motivation and performance was one factor that contributed to Robert's success. When his boss, a longtime practitioner of the approach, conducted his one-on-one session with Robert, he learned that his new employee had a confidence problem resulting from skill deficiencies, and, based on Robert's suggestion, he approved a series of training programs to equip Robert with the skills that he needed. Applying one of the basic tenets of the belief system, he knew that Robert would not be motivated unless he believed his efforts would lead to performance (Belief-1). Without confidence in themselves, this manager knew, employees won't try as hard as they can; in fact, they may not try at all.

The Value of Communication

If Robert's boss had not known about the belief system, there are other ways he could have learned that Robert felt troubled at work and suffered from a lack of motivation:

- *Behavioral analysis.* If he had observed Robert closely, he might have seen the behavioral manifestations of a confidence problem: Robert's anxiety, irritability, and his lack of concentration. He might have noticed that Robert wasn't using his time effectively, and that he wasn't putting in the effort needed to succeed at his job.

- *Skills analysis.* If he had carefully compared Robert's existing skills with those his new job called for, he would have uncovered a considerable skills gap. This might have led him to conclude that Robert needed new selling skills and that additional training was required for job success.

- *Organizational analysis.* If he had thoroughly reviewed his organization's hiring and training practices, he might have detected weaknesses in com-

Types of Motivation Problems		
B-1	**B-2**	**B-3**
Effort → *Performance* →	*Outcomes* →	*Satisfaction*
Lack of confidence	Lack of trust	Lack of satisfaction
"I can't meet the the performance expectations."	"Outcomes will not be tied to my performance."	"Outcomes will not be satisfy-ing to me."

pany policies and procedures. From this analysis, he might have concluded that Robert's skill deficiencies were overlooked when he was hired and that he was inadequately prepared for his new job.

But though these methods might have proved useful to Robert's boss, they are not infallible and can sometimes be misleading. It's not always easy, for instance, to interpret human behavior accurately or draw a clear connection between how an employee appears and what he or she feels. Nor will a skills analysis always lead you to the truth. For example, you may conclude that an employee has all the right skills for a job, but a B-1 problem may still exist if that employee believes the skills required are greater than they really are or is unsure about how well his or her skills measure up.

The belief system eliminates these misunderstandings and mistakes because it allows you to go directly to the source for the information you need. By requiring face-to-face communication with employees in a structured format, it ensures that you use the most reliable method for diagnosing motivation and performance problems. And by involving employees in the problem-solving process, it ensures that the solution you come up with is the one that is likely to work best.

DIAGNOSING AND SOLVING B-1 PROBLEMS

Dealing with B-1 problems, where employees lose motivation because they don't believe they can perform, doesn't have to be difficult or frustrating. Nevertheless, it often is, because managers don't always know how to solve them. Whether they carefully think through these problems or handle them on the spur of the moment, the result is often the same: Employees don't change much, nor does their motivation or performance.

At least part of the difficulty stems from not really knowing what to do. After all, it's not easy to influence employee beliefs, and because of their uncertainty about how to do it, managers tend to feel uncomfortable and at a disadvantage when they try. This holds managers back, causing them to ignore the problem. Or when they do take action, it's usually in the form of a pep talk: "You can do it" or "If you can't do it, I'm sure you can figure out how."

But solving B-1 problems doesn't have to be a guessing game. In most cases, the solutions they require are a natural and logical extension of their causes. And once you know that a B-1 problem exists and what's causing it, implementing a solution is usually easy. This structured approach—identifying the problem, determining its cause, and then selecting an appropriate solution—gives you a powerful yet practical way to manage employees whose motivation is suffering because they believe, "I can't do it."

Edward's Story

Edward G. had always been a high achiever and was normally self-confident. An account executive (AE) for more than five years, he knew how to take an account and run with it, and did everything he could to make a sale. When his company restructured and he was promoted to sales manager, he thought that his success was assured. But things didn't turn out that way and, for the very first time, Edward began to feel like a failure.

In the beginning, Edward felt he could master every aspect of his new position, including how to best manage his team of AEs. He applied a variety of management approaches with them. First, he tried the strategic approach: helping his people to develop sales strategies for each account. But he soon discovered that they didn't always execute well. Then he tried the "follow me" approach. But this didn't work either, because he ended up doing most of the work that his AEs were supposed to do themselves.

Though it helped them to sell more, this approach actually reduced their confidence level and motivation, and it took a heavy toll on Edward himself. It didn't take him long to realize that he couldn't keep going on every sales call with every AE on his team. Frustrated and depressed, Edward felt totally exhausted by the time his one-on-one session took place. He had tried everything he knew to steer his people in the right direction, but nothing was working and he didn't know where to turn.

Edward had a classic B-1 problem. His manager, Helen, was aware of his declining performance and strongly suspected that his confidence level was low. But she wasn't so sure that he would open up and discuss his situation. Would he admit his failure during their one-on-one session? Or would he deny his problems and continue on the same, confidence-draining path?

Questions for Diagnosing B-1 Problems

"Are things going all right?"

"Do you think you can complete this assignment?"

"Do you understand what to do?"

"How's your work coming along?"

"What do you think about our new performance standards?"

"Do you want me to work with you on this?"

"Have you done anything similar to this before?"

"Are you confident that you can handle this?"

"Do we require too much of you?"

When the session finally took place, Edward looked shaky and dejected, and the magnitude of his problems became clear. It took a lot of courage for him to open up and talk candidly with his manager—after all, Helen might turn against him, blame him for his problems, or refuse to provide support. But instead she understood the risk that he was taking and listened carefully so she could help in any way.

Edward's B-1 problem was really a skills issue. First, because he spent so much time coaching his AEs and assisting them on sales calls, he wasn't organizing his time well and couldn't focus on other parts of his job. Second, the management skills he applied with his AEs just weren't working. The two coaching approaches he tried had both failed, and he needed pointers in developing a more productive one.

During his session with Helen, Edward came up with two solutions to his B-1 problem. One was to schedule weekly meetings with her to review sales results and personnel issues, which he believed would help him to become more focused. Another was to solicit regular feedback from Helen about his coaching techniques and management skills. This might clarify what he was doing wrong with his AEs, he said, and help him develop review practices that would improve both their performance and his own.

Helen was receptive to Edward's suggestions and agreed to provide him with regular feedback. To fulfill her promise, she scheduled a weekly meeting for them on her To Do list, so they could review sales results, discuss personnel issues, and brainstorm ideas for improvement. In addition, she offered to conduct a workshop for sales managers, where they could exchange coaching and management techniques and help Edward determine the best way to work with his people.

Comments Indicating B-1 Problems

"There's no way I can increase sales by 75 percent."

"I'm not interested. I feel that I have about a one in ten chance of succeeding."

"You've got to be kidding. I don't think I can do that."

"I believe I have a 50–50 chance of pulling this off."

"I don't feel good about it. I might not be able to do it."

"That could happen, but it's not likely."

"I can't do it."

A Selection of B-1 Solutions

During her one-on-one session with Edward, Helen tried not to offer solutions to the issues that they discussed. Instead, she effectively applied one of the chief principles of the belief system: "If you want to know, ask." To help guide Edward to find solutions for himself, she posed probing questions to uncover problems, inquired about what their causes might be, and asked Edward outright what solutions might work best for him.

Though Edward's solutions were meant to address the specific problems he was experiencing, they were hardly unusual or difficult to implement. In fact, most of the solutions that managers and employees come up with to solve B-1 problems are easy to carry out and can be grouped into these categories:

- *Skill building*—using formal training to develop needed skills or providing coaching when employees can't be away from their job long enough to attend classroom training.
- *Job design*—changing job requirements, so that the skills needed for the job match those the employee already has.
- *Job transfer*—transferring the employee to another position, either within the unit or elsewhere in the organization, when skill building is too costly and job design is impractical.
- *Creating opportunities for success*—designing work situations that allow employees to practice required skills and develop proficiencies in areas where they lack confidence.
- *Providing adequate resources*—offering additional resources to raise employee confidence levels or show how to use existing resources more effectively.
- *Encouraging positive self-talk*—encouraging employees to avoid negative self-talk ("I'm a failure" or "Why can't I do anything right?") and carry on a positive internal dialogue ("I've succeeded at difficult jobs before; I know I can do it again").

DIAGNOSING AND SOLVING B-2 PROBLEMS

Like the B-1 problems described, B-2 problems are common and, at one time or another, show up in just about every business organization. After all, everyone has experienced the frustration of not getting what they rightly deserve: Good performance often goes unnoticed. It happens when promises are made but not kept, when managers don't have the authority to give employees what they deserve, or when organizations simply don't take care of their people.

The prevalence of performance-outcome problems, where employees believe "I will not get it," is widely acknowledged by managers, though many ignore their effect on motivation and performance or simply don't draw a connection. Consequently, these problems are frequently left unresolved, though their impact can be devastating. Once the bond of trust has been broken, it can take months or years to convince employees that outcomes are really tied to performance and that they can truly believe what their managers promise them.

Dr. B.'s Story

Situations like these are breeding grounds for the emotions that undermine employee commitment: cynicism, confusion, uncertainty, and disbelief. They can create such endemic mistrust that employees will often make assumptions that aren't true, compounding B-2 problems with problems that are either imaginary or based on misperceptions. The story of Dr. David B., a faculty member at a major university, is a case in point.

David was a well-known geneticist whose performance was widely recognized as being head and shoulders above everyone else in his department in terms of the three primary measures of academic performance: teaching, research, and service. But in the past, David's pay raises didn't always reflect his hard work, and there were years when he received no pay raise at all. One year, however, the chairman of David's department made sure that he received the largest salary increase of anyone on his staff. The next morning, David stormed into his chairman's office in a rage.

"When you told me about my raise, I was really excited," he said, "and I mentioned to everyone how pleased I was that this organization has finally become the kind of place where performance pays off. But I'm not sure I feel that way now, not after hearing that a couple of people got more money than I did. Everybody knows that they don't deserve it. So I guess I was wrong. Performance doesn't really count for anything around here."

As it turns out, the information that David received was incorrect. In reality, he *did* get the biggest raise in his department, but his organization's history of pay inequity had fueled his misperception and created a B-2 problem that shouldn't have existed.

Questions for Diagnosing B-2 Problems

"What do you think about the way people are treated here?"

"How do you feel about the way we reward performance?"

"What are your thoughts about the way rewards are tied to performance?"

"Do we follow through on our commitment to employees?"

"Do you believe that when employees produce more, they get rewarded for it?"

"Does it look as if everyone is treated the same here?"

How History Repeats Itself

If an organization has a history of B-2 problems, it can suffer setbacks in motivation when trying to launch a transformation effort. Why? Because organizations that change sometimes offer new incentives to motivate employees (stock options, profit sharing, etc.), but these incentives won't work if what has previously occurred leads employees to distrust or disbelieve what they're told.

This was precisely the situation that was encountered by an experienced production supervisor who we'll call Harold S. Working for a major manufacturing firm, Harold had considered moving to a lesser-known company but decided to remain when "a major new system" was announced in which everything would be based on performance. This would be a welcome change, Harold thought, especially for his people, who had long referred to their place of employment as "the hellhole." They had been treated poorly for such a long time, with low pay and poor benefits, that they felt management didn't care about them. Though they were capable of being productive—and wanted to—they never got rewarded when they were, and so they didn't really put out much effort to perform.

When the new system was implemented, Harold watched his people closely to see how they would react, but most of the time he saw nothing but doubt and skepticism on their faces. After two months, he still didn't notice any real improvement in their performance, even though there were signs that management was keeping its word and adhering to the new system. Despite the changes that were made, everyone seemed to have the same bad attitude they had before and kept on complaining about their company and their jobs.

Tying Outcomes to Performance

One lesson Harold learned from this experience is that it often takes a long time to raise B-2, particularly when there's a long history of performance-outcome problems. The most effective solution is the repeated tying of outcomes to performance, though this is not a solution that can produce immediate results.

With a few days of skill building, B-1 can go from low to high practically overnight. But this isn't the case when B-2s are low. Tie outcomes to performance once and employees will say, "That's only once." Do it a second time and they might say, "Two times doesn't mean things have changed." It may take three, four, or five times before you really change their minds and they begin to believe that outcomes are really tied to performance.

Comments Indicating B-2 Problems

"Promises. Promises. That's all we ever ge around here."

"Sometimes you get rewarded, sometimes not. You never know."

"Why work hard? Everybody gets treated the same."

"The union contract determines what you get, not how you perform."

"I've been promised a car for years, but nothing's happened."

"Why do a good job? They just pile on more work when you do."

Another reason B-2 problems are difficult to resolve is that managers don't always have complete control over outcomes; in most organizations, in fact, their authority to make pay and promotion decisions is limited. And when organizations change, promotions, raises, and bonuses can be severely curtailed, restricting management control over outcomes even further. In situations like these, managers who supervise employees with B-2 problems can honestly say, "There's nothing more I can do for you. My hands are tied."

Nevertheless, managers can minimize the damaging effects of B-2 problems by keeping these three points in mind:

1. *Focus on the outcomes you* can *control.* Rather than focusing on what you can't do, focus on the outcomes you do control. Every manager has control over some outcomes that employees want, like being kept informed,

having the opportunity to give input, being treated with respect, being appreciated, and so on.

2. *Most B-2 problems can be solved with simple, practical solutions.* When performance is good, offer employees something—anything, in fact—as long as it has value to them: praise, a word of thanks, or work that's more challenging or rewarding. Or withhold outcomes they find undesirable, like being yelled at, having to work the night shift, or having to travel a lot.

3. *Even B-2 problems that seem impossible to solve can be minimized.* When union contracts, corporate policy, or other factors prevent you from tying outcomes to performance, level with employees. Let them know that you can't give them what they want, but that you also won't tolerate their current performance and that you're willing to resort to drastic measures, like termination. In situations like these, when employees realize that they have few options, they often come to the realization that improving performance is in their best interest.

DIAGNOSING AND SOLVING B-3 PROBLEMS

Every manager has employees whose motivation and performance suffer because they're not satisfied with the rewards of their job. Though this situation is common, managers aren't always aware of it and, when left unaddressed, it can have negative long-term consequences. When B-3 problems persist, employees eventually feel cheated, become resentful, and begin to place blame.

Diagnosing B-3 problems—where employees are not getting the rewards they want most or are getting things they don't want—can sometimes be difficult, however. When asked, most employees will tell you if they like or dislike certain outcomes. But most won't readily volunteer this information because they're afraid their managers might use it against them. In change situations, employees become especially reluctant to voice dissatisfaction, because it puts them in the role of the "wet blanket." When their company is telling them that change is for the better, employees may think (but rarely say), "Better for the company, yes, but not necessarily better for me."

James's Story

This was the case with James H., a graduate of one of the country's top business schools, who interviewed with a prestigious consulting firm and was offered a position as a junior consultant. James gladly accepted, thinking it was the perfect job for him in this stage of his career. But when he reported for work, he was asked to shift into a position working on computer applications for clients.

Though James had serious reservations, he agreed to the change and threw himself wholeheartedly into his new duties. But eventually his enthusiasm began to wane, because the work he was required to perform wasn't really what he wanted to do. Instead of interacting with clients, he now found himself facing a computer all day long. And instead of the strategic and "big picture" issues he was hoping to focus on, he had to concentrate on the highly technical details of computer applications.

It wasn't long before James began to hate his job and the company that had hired him. He felt especially resentful because he believed he had been perfectly clear during his job interview about the kind of position he was looking for. "I want a job that allows me to work closely with people," he told the recruiter at that time, adding, "What I don't want is a technical job that requires precision or attention to detail or one that keeps me cooped up in an office."

Questions for Diagnosing B-3 Problems

"Do you enjoy the kind of work you're doing?"

"All things considered, are you happy with your job?"

"What specifically would you like to have that you're not getting now?"

"Could you tell me how you feel about your position overall?"

"Are you getting everything in your job that you need?"

"What are you getting from your job that you would rather not have?"

Offering Valued Outcomes

B-3 problems are common during change because the variables that define satisfaction in doing a job—the careful balance of variety, autonomy, and challenge—can suddenly be altered, and work that was once intrinsically rewarding can become dull or a struggle. What's more, the outcomes that employees have come to expect may have to be put on hold when a major organizational change takes place. For example, an employee who's been working diligently and has been promised a promotion learns that her company is "rightsizing" and that raises and promotions have been "frozen."

Even in the best circumstances, it's not always possible to give employees what they want most, which can lead to feelings of frustration and bitterness. But even in the worst circumstances, there are ways that you can increase job satisfaction and performance and minimize the negative feelings that accompany B-3 problems. These include the following:

- *Give valued outcomes.* If you're not sure what employees want, ask them. In most cases, you'll find, the rewards employees are looking for are outcomes you can easily deliver: recognition, increased feedback, or the chance to tackle a more challenging assignment.

- *Withhold undesired outcomes.* Sometimes you can improve motivation and performance simply by avoiding the outcomes that employees don't want: an increased work load, more authority, or out-of-town travel assignments.

- *Emphasize outcome drawbacks.* Employees often get hung up on outcomes that appear to be more desirable than they really are—a promotion that may require extensive travel and time away from home, for example. By helping them to see that they've overestimated the attractiveness of an outcome they desire, you may be able to eliminate it as an obstacle to improved motivation and performance.

- *Investigate alternative outcomes.* Finally, when you can't give employees what they expect or want most—or can't eliminate what they don't want—offer something to compensate for their disappointment. This may not generate the same level of enthusiasm or satisfaction, but it shows that you care, that you're sensitive to their needs, and that you're making an effort to meet them.

Comments Indicating B-3 Problems

"Things aren't the way I expect them to be."

"I'm not enjoying this as much as I expected."

"This is a great company, and I love my boss. But I don't enjoy my work anymore."

"I like my job, but I want more time for my family."

"If I can get that promotion, I'd be in heaven."

"Sometimes I just can't stand the thought of doing my job for even one more day."

In Chapter 4, we'll investigate the importance of teams in organizational change and how the belief system has been used to improve team motivation and performance.

4

Leading Teams to Change

Roy W. is not a big talker. Throughout the many years he worked for his company, he was never an active contributor in meetings. That's because Roy is basically more of a thinker than a talker: He pays close attention to what other people have to say and seriously thinks about it, but he only adds to the conversation when he feels a need to—and that's not very often.

Because he's a diligent worker and consistently achieves good results, Roy's unassuming nature and quiet ways had never caused him or his manager any problems. But when his company underwent a major restructuring a few years ago and instituted teams, Roy's reserved behavior suddenly became a workplace issue. Seemingly overnight, the other members of his team became highly critical of his lack of participation and began to complain that he was being "distant" and "aloof." Roy couldn't understand how they got that impression, and he felt hurt and confused by their accusations. Since he was never disinterested in meetings, he thought he was being unjustly criticized for taking his little "thinking trips" and for not speaking up more often. And since there had never been a problem with his performance before, he didn't know why he should have to change now.

Fortunately, Roy's manager, Joyce, routinely used the belief system approach, and in her one-on-one session with Roy she was able to clear up some of his confusion. She explained to Roy that because he expressed himself so infrequently in meetings he came across as remote to his team members and didn't appear to be a "team player." When you work in a team-based environment, she told him, you sometimes have to change how you act because people expect a certain kind of behavior.

Becoming a Team Player

Because she was asking Roy to do something that was unnatural for him, Joyce created the potential for a B-3 problem. After all, it wasn't that Roy lacked the skills or ability to speak up in meetings (that would be a B-1 problem); he simply was not a socializer and didn't like to talk much. If he did contribute more in team meetings, he believed, the outcomes he received would certainly be dissatisfying—namely, the discomfort, distress, and possible embarrassment that can accompany the act of talking in public.

With Joyce's probing, however, Roy was able to come up with a solution that he believed might work for him. After thinking over the situation carefully, he discovered that there were three satisfying outcomes to participation that might outweigh his natural dislike for it. First, Joyce would be happier if he contributed more, and that would be satisfying to him. Second, his team members would appreciate his contributions and show of interest and, therefore, might treat him better. And third, he would finally be recognized by his manager and his coworkers as the "team player" that everyone now expected him to be.

The one-on-one session worked for Roy because he realized that even though he can't change his basic nature or personal style he can change his behavior in certain situations in order to meet the expectations of others. And he developed a heightened awareness not only of his own personality, but also of how he appears to others and how they might misinterpret his demeanor.

Today, Roy works at the same company, though he has a different manager and serves on a different team. He still isn't the most talkative member of his group, but whenever there's a meeting, he speaks up every now and then—to ask a question or make a comment—even if it's only to signal to the others that he's interested in what's being said and that he wants to participate as a team player.

TEAMS AND ORGANIZATIONAL CHANGE

We included the story of Roy to demonstrate the importance of teams during organizational change and how the belief system can be applied to facilitate their introduction and improve their performance.

Teams are an integral component of just about every large-scale organizational change that occurs today. Whatever form they take—empowered, self-directed, crossfunctional, or project management—teams are often the most significant structural modification that organizations make when they change and the single most important factor in the success of a change effort.

When organizations restructure their workforce into teams, the results they achieve are sometimes remarkable. At the Westinghouse Electronic Assembly Plant in Texas, for example, empowered teams helped reduce cycle times for many products from twelve weeks to less than two. At Kodak's team-based customer service center, both employee productivity and first-time accuracy levels in helping customers with problems doubled. And at Texas Instrument's Defense System and Electronics Group, revenues per employee increased by 50 percent over a four-year period, largely as a result of new team structures.[1]

The Emotional Impact of Teams

Organizations that introduce teams don't always reap the benefits of increased teamwork, however; improvements in service, quality, and productivity are not guaranteed. Though teams can enhance organizational performance when implemented effectively, they also transform the interpersonal dynamics of the workplace and can create a host of entirely new organizational problems. There are several reasons why this can happen:

- *Effective teamwork requires high levels of motivation.* Teams don't work unless people are willing to collaborate and cooperate with each other, and this kind of close interaction requires trust, communication, and a willingness to resolve conflicts. Unless they're highly motivated, people may not invest the time and energy that's needed to build the stronger working relationships on which successful teams are based.

- *Teamwork intensifies the emotions associated with change.* Introducing teams during organizational change can increase the demands placed on people and exacerbate what is already a highly charged and emotional work atmosphere. Besides the increased expectations that normally come with change, team members feel the additional pressures of having to get to know each other better and work together more cohesively. "Intense daily contact on tasks and the constant thrashing out of differences of opinion place new demands on old relationships," says Deborah Harrington-Mackin in her book, *Keeping the Team Going.* "Walking away and ignoring each other are no longer acceptable options."[2]

- *Teamwork requires new styles of management and supervision.* Whenever teams are formed, the supervisory roles and relationships that had previously characterized the organization undergo significant alterations. In some cases, managers "manage" less and adopt more of a coaching role; in other cases, managers remain strongly involved with team members but engage in radically different activities: providing training to build self-management skills, for example, or acting as a mediator in team disputes. In every situation in which teams are introduced, however, the relationship between managers and their direct reports changes dramatically—and the adjustment involved can have emotional consequences.

When Teams Change Leaders

Another factor that complicates the emotional climate surrounding teams during change is that, given the high turnover rates now endemic in corporate life, teams are constantly being assigned new leaders. This can disrupt the stability of working relationships among team members and the delicate balance of power that it takes so long for teams to achieve, and it adds to the uncertainty that comes with organizational change.

The belief system can be instrumental in helping teams to overcome these challenges, because it compresses the time it takes for team members to get to know each other and provides a mechanism for maintaining good communication between teams and their leaders. When teams change leaders, the approach can also help uncover any residual motivation and performance problems that were left unresolved.

This was the case with a manager, who we'll call Scott P., who was hired to take over the department of someone in his company who retired. After only a few days on the job, Scott could tell that he was dealing with a team that had serious motivation problems: productivity levels were low, absenteeism was above average, and there was a noticeable lack of "team spirit." It seemed to Scott that these problems were especially pronounced among the female members of his new team, and he suspected the reason why.

Scott had heard stories about how unfair his predecessor had been to the first women employees he was forced by top management to hire. It took only a cursory review of departmental salaries to confirm that these stories were true. The first three women hired into the department earned considerably less than any of the men hired at the same time, Scott discovered, and also less than the women who were hired later. Though the three women had the same qualifications as their male peers— and seemed to be paid on the basis of their performance in recent years— they started out at lower salaries and didn't receive any raises during their first two years on the job. Apparently, Scott's predecessor had come to believe that women could perform as well as men, but he never corrected the pay inequity that he'd created so many years before.

When Scott conducted one-on-one sessions using the belief system approach, he wasn't surprised to find that the women on his team had low B-2s ("outcomes are not tied to performance"). As it turned out, however, the B-2 scores he recorded for the male members of his team weren't much higher. Though Scott hadn't anticipated this "spillover effect," it's actually quite common among employees who work on teams and are highly sensitive to pay and equity issues among team members.

Even when employees trust their organization and maintain high B-2 levels, inequities can weaken their belief about the performance–outcome relationship. Why? Because when employees with high B-2s see their coworkers being under–rewarded, they begin to think, "If it can happen to them, it can happen to me, too." With this realization usually comes a decline in B-2s, and motivation levels that were once high can take a turn for the worse.[3]

The Motivation Chain of Beliefs

B-1: "I can do it."

B-2: "Outcomes will be tied to my performance."

B-3: "Outcomes will be satisfying to me."

Once Scott understood what was causing the motivation problems on his team, he knew immediately how to improve the situation. He gave the three underpaid women a one-time increase to bring their compensation to an equitable level, and then made sure that he always tied outcomes to performance in the future. Though Scott had to justify his decision to his superiors to receive their approval, his actions over time had a positive impact on the motivation of his team and on their ability to work together as a cohesive unit.

TEAM TRANSFORMATIONS

Scott's story is just one of the many transformations that have occurred as a result of applying the belief system approach in a team setting. But we have another example that's even more illustrative of how this approach works with teams and how it can help managers to overcome one of the most common pitfalls of team leadership: applying a "blanket management approach."

Even leaders who subscribe to the principle that it's important to "manage to the individual" sometimes abandon this conviction when placed in a team setting. Despite their past success in managing one-on-one, they begin to think that being a team leader requires a more uniform approach and that they should manage their people not as individuals, but as a collective unit. In almost every case, however, this decision is a bad one and can lead to motivation and performance problems, as the following story shows.

The Manager as Military Leader

Howard S. was a sales executive in a large company who took over the leadership of his team during an organizational restructuring five years ago. At that time, Howard's team was one of the worst performing in the company, with sales revenues that placed it in the bottom quartile. This was unacceptable to Howard and, when combined with the rigors of organizational change, was enough to convince him to implement the belief system approach—a decision that helped initiate a remarkable journey of self-discovery for this manager.

A graduate of West Point, Howard was a seasoned business professional with many admirable qualities. He was intelligent, well organized, and highly competent, and wasn't afraid to tackle the most intractable business problems. Above all, Howard was determined to succeed, and he approached his job with a kind of gutsy resoluteness that you'd find in a dedicated military officer. Given the performance problems he faced, in fact, Howard felt that this kind of military approach to leadership was the most appropriate style for managing his team and that it should be applied uniformly with all team members.

But the impact that Howard's management style had on his team wasn't exactly what he intended. While he thought he was providing strong direction and leadership, most members of his team saw him in a completely different light: as critical, abrupt, unyielding, and abrasive. While he thought they welcomed the quick solutions he came up with for their problems, they resented his interference and unwillingness to consider their views. And while he thought they appreciated the consistency of his approach, most felt he didn't look at them as individuals or take enough time to understand their different needs.

What's more, Howard's hard-hitting style only added to the emotional turmoil that many of his team members felt as a result of the organizational changes they were going through. Instead of being more sensitive and accessible to his people during this difficult time, Howard actually became less so, firmly convinced that a "hands-off," sink-or-swim approach was the best way for them to learn how to adjust to change. Walking through the office briskly, he would bark orders, reprimand team members, and issue critical sales updates, all without breaking his stride.

Changes in Management Style

Needless to say, the feedback that Howard received during his one-on-one sessions came as somewhat of a shock. Not only had he greatly overestimated the benefits of his preferred leadership style, he'd also failed to realize how much his people looked to him for help and support and how much individual guidance they needed. Howard also learned that the blanket approach he was using to manage his team was generating numerous B-1, B-2, and B-3 problems.

By overlooking the individual needs of team members, for example, Howard had allowed some critical skill gaps to remain unfilled and this led to serious confidence problems (B-1). By managing his people as a unit, doling out praise and criticism without regard to individual performance, he gave some people reason to believe that they weren't being treated fairly (B-2). And by creating a wartime atmosphere at work, he took away the pleasure that people found in their work and deprived them of any job satisfaction that they previously derived from being in sales (B-3).

Though a few team members felt awkward about criticizing Howard in their one-on-one sessions, most took full advantage of the opportunity to voice the concerns and frustrations that had been building up inside them for months. One team member, in fact, had so much she wanted to get off her chest that she and Howard continued their session for nearly eleven hours, in a heated and sometimes highly emotional exchange of differing viewpoints.

As difficult as it was for Howard to hear some of this criticism, his need to succeed and sense of professionalism helped him to accept what his people were telling him and to implement some of the changes that they recommended. Though Howard couldn't change himself—his intense nature or hard-driving personality—he could change how he behaved, and these changes would have a significant impact on his team. Less than two years after implementing the belief system approach, in fact, Howard's team moved to the top quartile in sales revenues, landing the number-five position among similar teams in his company nationwide.

Howard's To Do List

1. Manage team members differently. Don't use a blanket approach to team leadership.
2. Use the right degree of hands-off management with each team member. Attempt a more hands-on approach, but vary it with each person and situation.

3. Drop the military approach; be more participative and less directive.

4. Make it easier for people to disagree with your solutions, and let people solve their own problems.

5. Shut up and listen. Seek more input from team members, and be more open to other points of view.

ENHANCING TEAM AWARENESS

The transformation that Howard and his team went through is not unusual. By applying the belief system approach to identify and solve motivation and performance problems, many teams in numerous organizations have achieved similarly impressive results. But this is not to suggest that all teams experience this process in the exactly same way, or that you can accurately predict the effectiveness of it in any given situation.

Just as the belief system acknowledges that people are unique and should be managed as individuals, it also recognizes the fact that people are unpredictable and sometimes react to this approach in ways that bring about little behavioral change or none at all. Yet even in these situations, the belief system often acts as a catalyst that can bring people to a new level of self-awareness and helps them to better understand the problems that they face.

Success or Failure?

The story of Steve R. illustrates what we mean. Steve was a sales executive at the same organizational level as Howard, the manager we just described, and worked in the same company. But in terms of management style and personality, Steve was unlike Howard in just about every way. Even tempered and easygoing, Steve was a pleasant and likable person, though almost too shy for someone in his position. Where Howard enjoyed the people part of his job, Steve preferred to spend most of the workday in his office, reviewing reports, calculating forecasts, and basically being alone.

You might think that compared to the militaristic style that Howard's team had to cope with the team members that Steve supervised would be grateful for his less-demanding approach. But in fact they found it to be quite frustrating and felt neglected by their manager. Because of the organizational changes they were going through, they wanted stronger support from Steve and more feedback. But these were activities that Steve, who treasured his self-imposed isolation, was reluctant to perform. Over time, the distant relationship that Steve maintained with his team resulted in significant B-1 and B-3 problems. Some team members felt they weren't getting enough coaching from their manager and needed more direction to do their job well (B-1). Others felt that the lack of management support made their job situation nearly intolerable, and that it was no longer possible for them to get any satisfaction from their work (B-3).

These were just a few of the complaints that Steve heard when he conducted his one-on-one sessions with his team. Among the others he received were "you don't spend enough time with us," "you procrastinate in helping to solve problems," and "you don't give us any feedback—positive or otherwise." The most difficult message Steve had to hear was the one voiced by virtually every team member: "I don't like this job, and I want another one." Most managers who go through the belief system process take comments like these to heart, and they begin to think about how they should change and manage differently. Even when they hear harsh criticism from subordinates, they're often grateful to learn how they come across to others and what they need to do to manage better. But Steve reacted in another way: He became defensive during his one-on-one and team sessions and refused to believe what his team members were telling him. Instead of acknowledging their concerns, he disagreed with what they said should be on his To Do list and discounted the emotional content of their messages.

Steve's To Do List

1. Give more feedback, reassurance, and coaching to team members.
2. Spend more time with the people on your team; get to know them better.
3. Don't procrastinate. When you spot a big problem, tackle it right away.
4. Use the right degree of hands-on management with each person, but vary it with each team member and situation.
5. Find out what people need by managing to the individual. Remember the belief system principle: If you want to know, ask.

In Steve's case, the belief system failed to bring about the behavioral changes that could have significantly improved relations with his team and enhanced his team's performance. But the process was not an entirely futile effort. At the very least, it increased awareness among team members of the kind of person their manager was, helped to rid them of false hopes, and allowed them to view their situation more rationally and less emotionally. Though some members of Steve's team did eventually leave and move on to other jobs, others decided to stay and confront the problems that the belief system had been instrumental in bringing to the surface.

In the following two chapters, we'll move beyond the subjects of individuals and teams and show what can happen when the belief system is applied with entire organizations.

NOTES

1. These and other examples of how companies have transformed themselves into effective team-based organizations are included in Richard S. Wellins, William C. Byham, and George R. Dixon, *Inside Teams: How 20 World-Class Organizations Are Winning Through Teamwork* (San Francisco: Jossey-Bass, 1994).

2. See Deborah Harrington-Mackin, *Keeping the Team Going: A Tool Kit to Renew & Refuel Your Workplace Teams* (New York: AMACOM, 1996), 114.

3. An even more damaging consequence occurs when employees with high B-2s see others being overrewarded. High B-2 employees may be getting what they deserve relative to their own performance, but relative to the overrewarded employees they may feel cheated. This causes them to think, "If they're getting that much, I should be getting more." Hence, they conclude, "I'm not getting what I deserve," and their B-2s begin to decline.

5

Leading Organizations to Change

About a year ago, a letter arrived at one of our offices from an executive who had used the belief system and was writing to offer his thanks. In the three years since he first introduced the approach in his organization, he wrote, his people achieved three consecutive years of financial results that far exceeded their targets, brought about the highest levels of customer satisfaction in the history of their division, and for the first time attained the status of "High Performance Team," a classification that his company used for internal benchmarking purposes. "While I'm sure that we all agree that there's never a simple answer to the complex motivation and performance problems that characterized this organization," he concluded, "our commitment to and investment in the belief system has been a key element of our success."

While this executive's letter provides a heartfelt testimonial to the power of the belief system approach, we mention it for another reason: It offers solid proof that the positive results that managers can achieve by applying this approach with individuals and teams, as we described in previous chapters, can also be achieved at the organizational level. When implemented consistently and effectively, the belief system can help turn around even the most troubled organizations, like the one led by the executive who wrote us this letter.

Emotional Scar Tissue

A man that we'll call Brad M., this executive was asked to take over the organization he managed—a large, geographically dispersed network engineering group—at a time when it ranked last in performance among all divisions in his company. To determine the underlying causes for this situation, Brad conducted an internal assessment with his leadership team and compiled a comprehensive organizational profile.

The report they produced described an organization that had hit rock bottom in terms of morale and motivation. After years of management neglect and abuse, the report stated, employees felt "disengaged, disempowered, and dispirited," their work atmosphere was characterized by "conflict, emotion, and scar tissue," and team spirit was practically nonexistent, with widespread "fear and insecurity influencing behavior."

Though many organizations continue to function under similarly dismal conditions, albeit producing mediocre or inferior results, Brad was determined to revitalize his group by providing the support they needed to improve their performance and by changing how they felt about their work. As he later said in his letter, "We committed ourselves as a leadership team to a simple principle: that if our people feel good about themselves and the work they do, results will take care of themselves." The tool that Brad chose to achieve this emotional revitalization was the belief system of motivation and performance.

From Analysis to Action

In the months that followed Brad's decision, a two-day training session in the belief system methodology was conducted for Brad's leadership team, followed by one-on-one sessions between Brad and his direct reports. These sessions, which uncovered significant B-2 and B-3 problems, provided important clues as to how the team had to proceed in order to bring about the organizational transformation they were seeking.

B-2 problems were pervasive, the sessions showed, because there was little apparent connection between how people performed and the outcomes they received. Everyone was treated essentially the same, it was believed: High performers were given no rewards for producing superior results, nor were there any adverse consequences for those who performed poorly. These beliefs, deeply ingrained after years of poor management, had undermined the organization's potential to become performance driven and created an environment in which the overall level of performance was substandard.

Motivating Employees to Perform

B-1		**B-2**		**B-3**
Effort	→ Performance →	Outcomes	→	Satisfaction

B-3 problems were also found to be common because people weren't getting the outcomes they wanted—like respect, support, and the authority to do their job well—and instead received many undesirable outcomes: fear of making mistakes, the stress of constant conflict, and the lack of management direction and support. In short, the oppressive work climate that had evolved over the years made it impossible for people to enjoy their work or the satisfaction that comes from doing a good job.

Based on these findings, Brad and his leadership team formulated a three-pronged organizational action plan:

1. Identify the B-3 problems that are unique to *each* employee and develop individualized action plans to resolve them.

2. Take action organizationwide on B-3 issues that were having a widespread negative impact, based on common themes that surfaced during the one-on-one sessions.

3. Work quickly to eliminate B-2 problems by immediately beginning the process of tying outcomes to performance and by consistently recognizing differences in work performance.

By implementing this simple action plan, Brad and his leadership team were able to undo the emotional damage caused by previous managers and, in one year's time, re-create their organization as a supportive, high-performance work culture. "In short," Brad later wrote in his letter, "we achieved the full turnaround and the revitalization that we were seeking when we met for the first time only three years ago."

IMPLEMENTING ORGANIZATIONAL SOLUTIONS

Applying the belief system with individuals and teams is almost always worthwhile, even when the results in improved motivation and performance are limited to the people directly involved in the process. But these benefits multiply exponentially when the approach is applied organizationwide and everyone participates to resolve problems that hinder work performance.

In many cases, in fact, an organizational application of the belief system is almost required because the factors that contribute to performance problems can only be dealt with on an organizational level.

Consider the manager who uncovers extensive B-1 problems among the people on her team, for example, because they lack the skills they need to achieve expected results. How can she help her people acquire those skills if her organization does not allocate funds for ongoing training and development?

Organizational applications of the belief system are also necessary when motivation and performance problems are rooted not in the actions of a single manager or leadership team, but in a work culture that has persisted for years or survived several management generations. In these cases, isolated applications of the approach may help to solve immediate problems or bring about local improvements, but they cannot address the organizational factors that strongly influence those problems and that, if left unchanged, may cause them to recur.

Applying the belief system organizationwide is, of course, more difficult, time consuming, and costly than individual or team applications. But when the problems that need to be solved are largely the result of organizational factors, the time, energy, and financial investments are well worthwhile. All things considered, the organizational approach may be the most cost-effective way to improve motivation and performance and the only sure way to achieve lasting change.

When Culture Hinders Change

The introduction of the belief system several years ago in the sales division of a telecommunications company provides a good example of the benefits to be derived from organizational applications. Like others in this newly deregulated industry, this company was trying to make the adjustment to a new and more competitive marketplace. But the culture the company had long maintained was impeding its progress and significantly hindered its attempts to achieve permanent change.

A review of the division's sales statistics confirmed our initial impression that this was not a culture that promoted or encouraged high performance. Though there were almost one hundred salespeople in the division, covering sales territories that spanned five states, not one salesperson was meeting quota in all ten or so products marketed by the company. Though a few salespeople were meeting quota in two or three products, only a handful were meeting quota in most of them.

In addition, management had allowed this low level of performance to continue for some time. Many salespeople, we discovered, had *never* met quota for products they'd been selling for as long as three years, and there never seemed to be any adverse consequences for poor performance. Turnover in the division was quite low, in fact, and most people were kept on in the same capacity for years, no matter what their sales results.

Why was this kind of work behavior tolerated? One reason was that the company had historically faced little competition in its field; therefore, it developed a culture over time that more closely resembled that of a governmental agency than a business organization. Raises and promotions were based more on job tenure than job performance, and management functioned with a bureaucratic mindset: As long as employees followed the organization's rules, policies, and procedures, they never had to worry about losing their status or their job.

Achieving Cultural Turnaround

Application of the belief system approach revealed that there were many motivation and performance problems that had to be resolved before this division could become a competitive, performance-based organization.

B-1 problems, for example, were commonplace; since salespeople weren't held accountable for their performance, many never bothered to develop the skills they needed to achieve better results. B-2 problems were widespread, because outcomes had never been tied to performance—an unfortunate precedent that had been set by management many years earlier. And though you might think that a permissive culture like this one would be conducive to job satisfaction, there were also many B-3 problems. The ongoing lack of achievement counteracted any positive feelings people had about their work, and many people were mismatched with their jobs. Since results were not a major concern of management, little attempt had been made to ensure the right organizational fit for employees, so many found their jobs to be intrinsically dissatisfying.

Based on these findings, a comprehensive improvement plan was drawn up that included these action steps:

- Work with salespeople to overcome their B-1 problems by providing additional coaching and sales training and by enhancing their product knowledge.
- Strengthen B-2 beliefs ("outcomes are tied to performance") by clearly communicating sales targets to employees and by taking appropriate measures when those targets are not met. These included establishing development plans for poor performers, setting time frames for bringing individual performance up to target levels, and terminating employees who consistently failed to meet performance targets.
- Improve job satisfaction (B-3) by providing the support salespeople required to achieve success in their jobs—and feel good about them—and by moving people out of jobs that they were either unqualified for or temperamentally unsuited to perform.

Cultural Transformation

Before the belief system	After the belief system
Bureaucratic mindset	Business mindset
Complacent attitude	Competitive attitude
Tenure driven	Performance driven
Rules focused	Results oriented

Less than a year after implementing this plan, the division reported results that were nothing less than startling, given its past performance. For the entire range of products marketed by the company, sales revenues averaged 20 percent *above* quota, and for one product reached nearly 300 percent of quota!

These results could not have been achieved by applying a piecemeal approach to motivation and performance improvement. Implementing the belief system with individuals or teams would not have been a useless endeavor (it may have created pockets of improvement, for example, that could have served as models for others in the organization). Only by applying the approach organizationwide could the division resolve systemic problems and create the kind of culture that would allow it to become truly competitive.

A TOOL FOR ORGANIZATIONAL ANALYSIS

On the surface, any organizational application of the belief system may seem to contradict the very principles on which the approach is based. According to the belief system, after all, motivation and performance problems are unique to individuals and can only be solved satisfactorily between managers and their direct reports. This is the primary function of the one-on-one session, as you may recall, and the rationale for involving employees in finding solutions to motivation problems. How is it possible, then, to devise strategies to improve motivation and performance based on the belief system approach that will be effective organizationwide? And when managers apply these organizational improvement strategies, don't they end up ignoring precisely those individual situations that the belief system is designed to address?

The answer is that the belief system can work effectively on both levels—with individuals and organizationwide—even at the same time. While it's true that the problems that the approach uncovers reflect the unique circumstances and work situation of each employee, those circumstances are often similar for many employees in the same organization. This is especially true when the circumstances that impact motivation and performance problems are shaped by leaders who make decisions that apply organizationwide.

Anticipating B-1, B-2, and B-3 Problems

It's not surprising, for example, to find similar B-1 problems among employees if they work in an organization that provides no training and routinely neglects the development of its people. When leaders regularly fail to tie outcomes to performance, the people they manage tend to develop B-2 issues. Even B-3s, the most idiosyncratic among the three types of motivation problems, usually demonstrate more consistency within an organization than you might expect.

Types of Motivation Problems

- Lack of confidence (B-1): "I can't meet the performance expectations."
- Lack of trust (B-2): "Outcomes will not be tied to my performance."
- Lack of satisfaction (B-3): "Outcomes will not be satisfying to me."

Naturally, some employees may desire outcomes that no one else in their organization may need or want. A parent with a troubled teenager, for example, may believe that she requires more flexible work hours as a condition for job satisfaction in order to spend more time at home. Or an employee with peculiar work habits may request a special seating arrangement or office. But in most cases the B-3 problems that surface during one-on-one sessions demonstrate a discernible pattern. In organizations where managers treat their people abusively, for instance, "respect" is often one of the outcomes that employees will say they need most. When organizations fail to communicate with their people, "being kept informed" is an outcome that many of their employees will say they require in order to be happy at work. Or when organizations rely strictly on authoritarian management practices, employees will often voice the desire for a more participative work environment.

Predicting Performance Problems

This means is that the belief system can serve as a valuable tool for organizational analysis, even without the implementation of training sessions, one-on-one meetings, and team meetings. Though the regenerative power of the approach increases significantly when it's implemented in this way (see Chapters 8 to 13), the belief system model can also be used to predict and prevent performance problems—and effectively guide management decision making—without conducting extensive data gathering or in-depth employee interviews.

The work that one of us conducted with an insurance company several years ago demonstrates this point. This company, one of the largest in its industry, was planning a major organizational change that involved job redesign in two critical functions: customer service and case work. The objective of the change effort was to shorten the time it took to resolve customer problems, which in the past had involved employees from both departments.

Traditionally, the main job of the customer service agents was to take calls from customers with problems or complaints, gather any relevant information about the problems from customers, and turn this information over to a department staffed with case workers. These back-office professionals would then analyze and research the problems they were handed, decide how to resolve them, and call back the customers to relay their decisions. The employees who worked in these two functions were as different as night and day. The customer service agents tended to be friendly, easygoing people who demonstrated superior interpersonal skills as well as a warm and caring attitude with customers. The case workers, on the other hand, were hard-charging, decisive problem solvers who focused primarily on resolving issues as quickly as possible. The job redesign called for the merger of these two positions; each employee, in other words, would perform both functions for a single customer.

Though neither of us was directly involved in this change effort, one of us was working with the vice president of the company at that time, who asked, "Would you mind telling us what you think about this planned change? Will the job redesign work?"

It's unlikely that the change effort will succeed, the analysis said, because it will create extensive B-1 problems. The customer service agents are not equipped to handle the case worker functions, and the case workers are a mismatch for the customer service job. If the change is implemented, chances are most of these employees will feel overextended and overwhelmed. "I'm comfortable carrying out some of these functions," they will say, "but I can't handle all of them."

The analysis also pointed out that training would probably not rectify this situation. The two functions call for radically different personality types, and few people embody both. Those who are good at interacting with customers tend not to be hard-charging problem solvers, and vice versa. It's simply unrealistic to expect these employees to master a position that requires such a wide range of capabilities and skills.

Because of this, the report also predicted that the change effort would create numerous B-3 problems. Since no one likes to perform work they're not suited for, most employees would experience considerable job dissatisfaction in the redesigned position. Some employees might find parts of the new job satisfying, but the dissatisfying parts would carry a heavier weight, and the result would be widespread motivation and performance problems.

In conclusion, the analysis recommended that the company halt the redesign project and rethink the entire change effort. While logical from a work-flow point of view, the analysis said, the planned reorganization failed to take into consideration the human element and the negative emotions that would accompany the change.

About six months later the vice president who received this analysis called to say that her company had proceeded with the job redesign and that it had, indeed, turned out to be a disaster. How did their employees react to the change? "They told us exactly the same thing you did in your analysis," she admitted. "At the time, we saw it as complaining. But now we wish we had listened to them—and to you."

Organizational Analysis Using the Belief System Model

To identify potential B-1 problems, ask

Does the organization provide frequent, high-quality training to all employees?

Is the organization growing too rapidly for employees to receive the training or resources needed to do their job adequately?

Is technological change proceeding at a pace that requires the constant upgrading of skills?

To identify potential B-2 problems, ask

Do managers consistently tie outcomes to performance?

Does the organization require managers to measure employee performance and apply those measures to pay and promotion decisions?

Does inequity in outcomes exist among employees?

To identify potential B-3 problems, ask

What outcomes would employees like the organization to provide?

To what extent are desirable outcomes available to employees?

Do employees received outcomes that may be considered undesirable?

Facilitating Successful Change

The application of the belief system to a change initiative at a major hotel company some years ago also demonstrates the validity of this model for organizational analysis. In this case, however, the recommendations in the analysis that was submitted were accepted by the organization's managers and helped them to achieve more positive results.

Though this company owned and operated hotels under its name, the focus of its business for many years had been on franchising its name to hotel operators with their own properties. Then the business strategy of the company changed, reverting back to a focus on managing company-owned hotels, but it was unclear whether the company was operationally equipped to carry it out effectively.

The unit that was responsible for opening new hotels knew full well that they no longer possessed the expertise that was required to make the change succeed. It didn't make sense to invest millions of dollars in new properties and then make mistakes in opening the hotels or, even worse, run the risk of delayed openings, which might cost the company millions more. To find out what was needed to ensure a successful launch for the new hotels planned, the company requested an organizational analysis based on the belief system model.

In the analysis that was submitted, no B-2 or B-3 problems were anticipated during the change effort, based on what was known about the company and how it was managed. But the analysis warned of potentially serious B-1 problems if the skills needed to open the new hotels could not be acquired or developed. There were four possible solutions presented:

1. Recruit people internally with previous experience in opening hotels.
2. Train existing managers in the skills needed to open new hotels.
3. Assemble a team of managers who are fast learners and willing to struggle through the hotel-opening process.
4. Hire a consulting firm that specializes in providing assistance to companies that open hotels.

In reviewing this list, the company's leaders decided to eliminate the first option because most of the managers with the experience needed were unavailable: Many had moved up to become executives, some had relocated to manage company properties in foreign countries, and others were working for competitive organizations or had retired. The second and third options were also rejected. There was no one internally who could provide training in the skills that were needed, and the company was unwilling to accept the risks involved in having unskilled managers open new hotels. Though these managers might benefit from the experience as a learn-as-you-go process, the mistakes they might make along the way could be serious and result in costly delays.

In the end, the leaders of the company decided to implement the final proposed solution. This option would allow them to acquire the skills they needed to open the new hotels that were planned and, by having their managers work alongside the consultants, to develop the needed skills for any future hotel openings.

In the next chapter, we'll look at additional applications of the belief system model to show how it can drive effective management decision making and facilitate change.

6

Managing Routine Organizational Change

In the early 1980s, a company that delivered government-funded training programs was experiencing many of the problems that beset organizations undergoing fast growth. One of the most troublesome was the need to find qualified, experienced trainers who could perform their jobs competently right from the start and help the company fulfill its contractual obligations. The rapid rate at which the company was expanding afforded little room for error in making hiring decisions. Managers had no time to coach new trainers, and allowing them to learn "on the job" was too risky. What the company needed was an effective selection strategy that would guarantee the right skills and confidence levels in new trainers at the time they were hired. By establishing such a hiring process, the company would ensure high B-1 levels in all new trainers ("I can do it"), and reduce the likelihood of costly motivation and performance problems later on.

In a short time, the company came up with a selection strategy that worked nearly perfectly, helping its managers to efficiently sift through the hundreds of applicants who responded to advertisements for the trainer position. Unlike traditional selection techniques, which rely strongly on face-to-face interviews, the one this company created focused instead on assessing skill levels. This is how it worked.

Assuring High B-1s

All applicants for the trainer position were given twenty minutes to review the company's trainer manual and prepare to conduct a short training session. Then each was scheduled a time to return and conduct the session while being videotaped. During these taped sessions, three of the company's managers acted as trainees to test the applicants' skills in teaching the program material and assess their ability to handle typical training room situations.

A self-selection process began almost immediately. Applicants who believed "I can't do it" withdrew themselves from consideration early on, either before they received the trainer manual or before their scheduled taping. There were several reasons why these applicants decided to leave: Some felt they didn't have the skills required for the job, for example, while others were uncomfortable with the idea of being taped. The majority of those who remained tended to have good training skills and reasonably high B-1 levels.

The videotapes of these applicants were then evaluated by a group of staff members that included key managers from the company's headquarters who were not present at the taped sessions. Through these evaluations, it was possible to make a fairly accurate determination as to who was right for the trainer job and who wasn't. But the selection process didn't end there.

Those who demonstrated the strongest skills in this smaller pool of applicants were then offered the opportunity to attend sixty hours of train-the-trainer sessions, where they practiced the skills required for the job and received intensive feedback. Once again, self-selection took place, as applicants developed a greater awareness of what the job they were applying for entailed and whether or not they felt they could do it.

By the time this training was completed, the number of job applicants had dwindled considerably, but these were the ones that the company knew were the best hiring prospects. Everyone in this group, especially those who were finally offered the position, knew they had the skills and the confidence to perform well as trainers. Without a doubt, each one had both the ability and the motivation to carry out the responsibilities that the job required; each one possessed a strong belief that "I can do it."

A Tool for Decision Making

This selection strategy continued to serve the company well for a number of years. For one large government contract, in fact, the company used it to hire 160 trainers in a two-week period. From that group, one trainer was later terminated, for reasons unrelated to his training skills. But the other 159 stayed on with the company and performed well for the duration of the contract.

The point we're trying to make with this example is probably obvious to you by now: As a tool for management decision making, the belief system approach can be effective not only in companies that undertake large-scale change, but also in those that must cope with change on a regular or daily basis. Even when change is small, incremental, or episodic, leaders can prevent or resolve motivation and performance problems caused by change—and minimize the negative emotions associated with them—by applying the belief system model.

The Belief System Model

"People are motivated by what they believe."

B-1	**B-2**	**B-3**
Effort →	*Performance* →	*Outcomes* → *Satisfaction*
"I can do it."	"Outcomes will be tied to my performance."	"Outcomes will be satisfying to me."

In later chapters, we'll present case studies that demonstrate how the belief system model was implemented to help two large organizations carry out major change initiatives. In both examples, we'll show how the belief system was "cascaded" throughout each organization using training sessions, one-on-one sessions, and team sessions, and how the approach helped to resolve specific motivation and performance problems that were caused by the change event.

But in this chapter our focus is somewhat different. Here, the applications we present will illustrate how managers have used the belief system approach to guide their decision making in routine change situations like those related to hiring, promotion, development, or termination. All the examples we'll provide come from the same business organization, the one that came up with the unique selection strategy that we have described.

This organization did not undertake any major change initiatives throughout the 1980s; it was never restructured, reengineered, or "rightsized." But because of its fast growth and rapid expansion, change was a factor that its managers had to deal with repeatedly. In this regard, it was similar to many companies today, which operate in a highly competitive business environment and a global economy that forces them to adjust, adapt, and change almost continuously.

LOOKING AT PROBLEMS IN NEW WAYS

Managers who adopt the belief system model as a decision-making tool learn to look at change-related problems in new ways. In most cases, this helps them to develop better solutions because the approach provides an effective framework for analysis, one that allows them to examine the three factors that are critical to motivation and performance: confidence, trust, and satisfaction. The example of a promotion decision in the organization we mentioned will show what we mean.

Dewitt M. was a longtime employee in sales support whose performance had always been exceptional. Consequently, his manager, faced with a pressing need for additional salespeople, was thinking about promoting him into a direct-sales position. There's nothing unusual, of course, about a manager suggesting this kind of job change for an employee. In many companies, production workers who perform well move up to become production managers, and top salespeople are frequently promoted into sales management. Nevertheless, Dewitt's manager decided to wait before making his final decision, and these are the thoughts that went through his mind.

As far as his work in sales support is concerned, this manager thought, Dewitt performs well and is highly motivated. He does good work and he knows it, so his B-1 level is probably very high. On a scale of 0 to 10, in fact, his B-1 score would total at least 9. But what would be Dewitt's B-1 score if he were promoted into direct sales?

B-1 Analysis: Dewitt in Sales Support										
0	1	2	3	4	5	6	7	8	**9**	10
I cannot perform as expected.					*Not sure.*				*I can perform as expected.*	

This question prompted the manager to conduct an analysis to compare Dewitt's selling skills to those that would be required for his new sales job, and he discovered that Dewitt lacked two or three of the most essential ones, a fact that Dewitt himself confirmed. Though Dewitt was capable and confident in his current sales support position, his B-1 score after his promotion would probably plummet. As long as he lacked the skills that he'd need to succeed in his job, Dewitt would believe "I can't do it," and he wouldn't be motivated to perform. In this case, using the belief system approach helped this manager avoid one of the most common mistakes that are made in promotion decisions: assuming that employees who perform well in one position have the skills and confidence required for success in positions at a higher level.

B-1 Analysis: Dewitt in Direct Sales

0	1	**2**	3	4	5	6	7	8	9	10
I cannot perform as expected.					*Not sure.*			*I can perform as expected.*		

Why Mindy Failed to Perform

As the two examples we've provided so far show, it helps to conduct a B-1 analysis whenever you hire someone who's completely new to a job or when you shift an employee into a totally new position. But an analysis like this may also be useful even when the job changes an employee must make seem relatively minor.

Remember, if an employee has performed the same work well before—using the same skills, resources, and procedures and under the exact same circumstances—you have no reason to suspect that a B-1 problem will occur. But when a job becomes different in any way, then you must be alert to potential B-1 problems. The story of Mindy W., another employee in the training company we've been discussing, illustrates this point and how important it is to conduct a thorough analysis when assessing B-1 levels.

When Mindy was hired to fill a key sales position in this company, she seemed to be perfectly suited for the job. All the information her manager collected about her before and during her interview indicated that he had made an excellent choice. Mindy was highly enthusiastic about working for her new company, appeared to have all the skills required for the sales position, and maintained an outstanding record of performance in previous sales jobs. The manager who hired Mindy was also determined to provide her with all the support and resources she would need to succeed. She was given a large support staff, a big budget, and unlimited access to her manager, a seasoned sales professional who was intimately familiar with her territory and eager to help out in any way that he could.

Only a month after Mindy was hired, however, her manager realized that he had made a serious mistake. Not only were Mindy's initial sales results abysmal, her attitude toward her new job soured almost immediately. She began arriving late to work each morning, barely spoke to her coworkers and staff, and cancelled appointments with some of her most important prospects. There were even times when Mindy became highly emotional in the office and seemed to be on the verge of tears. It was clear that Mindy was giving up. She didn't seem to possess the skills or confidence to do her job well; she no longer maintained a strong belief that "I can do it."

At first, Mindy's manager didn't understand what was causing Mindy's B-1 problem, but after accompanying her on some sales calls and talking with prospects she had approached, the cause of her problem eventually came to light. As it turned out, Mindy lacked a critical skill in performing her job: identifying and overcoming buyer objections. Because of her successful job history, it seemed natural to assume that Mindy had mastered this skill, but it was wrong for Mindy's manager to make that assumption.

In her new job, Mindy was selling a different product to buyers who were at a higher organizational level than those she had sold to in the past, and they intimidated her. As a result, she found it difficult to overcome their objections and concerns during sales calls, and this change alone was enough to undermine the confidence she demonstrated when she was first hired. Though the differences between Mindy's previous jobs and her new one may seem relatively minor to us, they appeared as major obstacles to Mindy and had a devastating impact on her motivation and performance.

A FRAMEWORK FOR DAILY DECISION MAKING

Over time, managers who adopt the belief system approach as a way of managing change begin to develop a particular mindset. Whenever they make decisions at work, they automatically think in terms of the three beliefs that the approach is based on and how their decisions will impact them. In most cases, the management decisions that are reached in this way lead to stronger B-1s, B-2s, and B-3s among employees, and to higher levels of motivation and performance. An example of this kind of decision making follows.

Elmer's Rewards

Turner S., a manager in the same training company we've been discussing, had been trying for weeks to finalize a half-million dollar contract to provide training for a state agency. Before entering into the contract, the top officials at the agency wanted to make sure they had the support of key managers from around the state; these were the managers who would be sending their people to the training sessions. Even though they had met with these managers several times to explain the program, the agency officials were having trouble getting the managers to endorse the training contract. To resolve this situation, Turner suggested inviting the managers to attend a one-hour segment of the training so that they could experience the program firsthand. The agency officials agreed that this would be an excellent way for the managers to reach an informed decision.

Five members of Turner's staff were present on the day the managers showed up. These included Higgins, Turner's best project leader, who outlined the goals and purpose of the demonstration; Elmer, Turner's most experienced trainer, who conducted the sample training; and three assistants, to set up the seminar room for the demonstration and make sure the invited managers felt comfortable. Everyone on Turner's staff who was present that day did a outstanding job, but Elmer stole the show by conducting a flawless sample training session that resulted in the managers' overwhelming endorsement of the contract. Though Elmer had always been an above-average performer, his work was truly exceptional that day, and the contract was signed the following week.

Turner had always praised Elmer for his good work in the past, but he wanted to do something special to acknowledge the extra effort Elmer had put in to win the agency contract. After all, Elmer had been willing to take on a high-pressure assignment, spent time after work to prepare and rehearse for the presentation, and still managed to keep up with his regular duties. Tuner decided to give three outcomes that he knew were important to Elmer: praise, recognition, and money.

The Value of Positive Reinforcement

How much of each outcome was appropriate? Turner decided that he would give Elmer (1) the highest praise possible, (2) public recognition for his contribution, and (3) a $2 thousand cash bonus. The day following the agency presentation, Turner called the five staff members together and thanked each one for their contribution in helping the company to land the state contract. Then he turned to Elmer and said, "The training you did was the best I have ever seen. It couldn't have been better, and it impressed the group immensely. Thank you again for all your hard work."

When the contract was signed, Turner sent out a memo to everyone in the training unit and to all managers in the chain of command, including the president. Though the names of all five staff members were mentioned in the memo, a full paragraph was devoted to Elmer's performance and to the critical role it played in winning the state contract. This made Elmer something of a company celebrity for a few days afterward, and he received a lot of attention from his coworkers, as well as some congratulatory handshakes from several higher-ups.

Given the widespread recognition of Elmer's contribution, Turner had no problem getting approval from his superiors for the $2 thousand cash bonus. And when he handed over the check to Elmer, he made it a point to recap the highlights of Elmer's performance, to make sure Elmer knew exactly what the bonus was for.

Turner had good reasons for acknowledging Elmer's performance in the ways that he did. The first was that he truly felt Elmer deserved the praise, the recognition, and the bonus that he received. The second was that by tying outcomes directly to performance and by offering outcomes that he knew were wanted Turner made sure that Elmer's B-2 and B-3 beliefs remained strong during a time of rapid change for the company and that his motivation to perform well remained high. In addition, as a result of this positive reinforcement and the way it was handled, B-2 levels throughout the company increased substantially because everyone was able to conclude, "If you do a good job here, it really pays off."

A TOOL FOR MANAGEMENT LEARNING

Using the belief system as a tool for making change-related decisions is a good way to prevent motivation and performance problems. But even when managers make bad decisions related to change, the approach can serve as a useful framework for analyzing what went wrong and helping managers to learn from their mistakes. To understand how, consider the story of Kevin and Jay, two other training company employees.

The Story of Kevin and Jay

When Kevin started working at the company, he had just graduated from college and was only twenty years old, but he was mature for his age and his performance was exceptional. In addition, as a number of managers noted, he was the kind of worker that you could give an assignment to and know it would be done well without ever having to check on him.

Jay, an extremely competent middle manager who everyone agreed was on the way up, wanted Kevin to work in his department, and he talked to Kevin about it. During this meeting, Kevin was very clear about what he wanted in a job and what he needed to perform at his best. There were four outcomes that Kevin specifically mentioned: (1) opportunities for growth and development, (2) frequent interaction with his manager, (3) detailed feedback on his performance, and (4) recognition when he performed well.

With Jay's assurance, Kevin applied for the job change and began to work in Jay's department. Once again, his performance was outstanding—at least at first—and he seemed to need practically no management supervision. This was a quality that Jay appreciated immensely, because he was responsible for a major profit center and enormous demands were placed on his time.

Jay would meet with Kevin occasionally, however, usually when he wanted to give Kevin additional work or ask him to take on a new assignment. Since he knew these assignments were important to Kevin, he always made sure to select ones that would be interesting and challenging and that would allow Kevin to acquire new skills and experience.

Jay was somewhat hurt and surprised, therefore, when he found out a few months later that Kevin had gone to the personnel department and asked for another position. Hadn't he offered Kevin a job that would help him to grow and develop? And hadn't he provided the professional challenges that Kevin was looking for?

To find out what went wrong, Jay decided to apply the belief system approach and analyze Kevin's B-1, B-2, and B-3 levels. When he constructed charts to perform this analysis (see Chapter 2), he could detect no serious problems with Kevin's B-1 or B-2. But his analysis of Kevin's B-3 level showed a different story.

Belief System Analysis: Kevin's B-3			
−10 −8 −6 −4 **−2** 0 +2 +4 +6 +8 +10			
Outcomes dissatisfying	*Outcomes slightly dissatisfying*	*Outcomes slightly satisfying*	*Outcomes satisfying*

When he thought back on the outcomes that Kevin had said he wanted, Jay realized that he'd neglected to provide most of the ones that were most important to Kevin. Jay, in fact, had provided Kevin with only one of them—opportunities for growth and development— while ignoring the other three. This meant that the satisfaction Kevin thought he would receive from his job fell far short of what he had hoped for. Consequently, his B-3 level was probably quite low, Jay realized, only as high as a low positive rating (in the +1, +2, +3 range), and probably even lower (in the -1,-2, -3 range).

Learning to Change

The lesson that Jay learned from conducting this analysis was too late to save his relationship with Kevin, and he lost a valued employee.

But you can be sure that he tried not to make the same mistake again, and that he worked harder from then on to provide whatever outcomes that his employees told him they wanted.

In situations like this one, where the manager is the primary cause of the motivation problem, the belief system approach often serves as a catalyst for personal change. Even when the immediate problem cannot be corrected or reversed, just by applying the approach in trying to understand it can heighten the manager's self-awareness and prevent similar problems from recurring. The story of Robbie K., a supervisor at the training company, exemplifies this point.

Known companywide for his phenomenal word processing skills, Robbie had been promoted to head of his department, where he established the same rigorous standards for his subordinates that he used to strive to meet. Whenever he hired new workers, in fact, he tended to select overachievers like himself, whose B-1 levels were little affected by his high expectations. But some of the operators who had been working in the department before Robbie's promotion, especially those with merely good or average skills, were beginning to have some problems.

Mary, who had been with the company for several years, was included in this group. Though she was a competent word processor, her performance never seemed to be good enough for Robbie. The ultimate perfectionist, he kept pushing his people to adopt new ways of working so they could perform better, and he worked with them individually to improve their proficiency. But if they didn't do the work "right," according to his elevated standards, he'd ask them to do it over again and again.

After having to deal with Robbie's "it's never good enough" management style day in and day out, Mary concluded exactly what you'd expect: "No matter how much I try, I can't do what Robbie expects." Her B-1 level gradually declined until it was practically 0 ("I cannot perform as expected") and, of course, her motivation went with it.

Mary's B-1 Analysis										
0	1	2	3	4	5	6	7	8	9	10
I cannot perform as expected.					*Not sure.*			*I can perform as expected.*		

Robbie was, of course, very much aware of his perfectionist tendencies; they were, in fact, a source of great pride to him. But he wasn't aware of the harmful impact they were having on the people he managed. Like many others in comparable positions, Robbie incorrectly assumed that what had motivated him would also motivate his subordinates. But it actually had the opposite effect: Instead of achieving improved productivity and quality, the performance of his department started to decline.

Conducting a B-1 analysis for Mary's motivation problem would have alerted Robbie to the stylistic changes he needed to make. Certainly, those changes would have been difficult for him; lowering expectations and becoming less of a perfectionist are not easy adjustments. But by using the belief system approach, Robbie would have recognized the source of the problem and the need to change—and that would have been a critical first step to improving Mary's motivation problem.

_____ PART III

APPLYING THE MODEL
TO LARGE-SCALE CHANGE

7

Systematic Applications and Implementation Strategies

A few years ago, on the last day of a training session to introduce the belief system approach, a manager who was attending related a story. One of the people on his staff, a bright, young project coordinator, had come to him with a problem some months earlier. She was uncomfortable in her new job assignment, she said, and was feeling very discouraged. "I'm floundering in this position," she said in a quivering voice, "and I don't think I can do it anymore." Impressed with her honesty and directness, the manager wanted to offer some help. Quickly, he concluded that what she needed was a little encouragement. So he gave her a spirited pep talk, assuring her that things would get better and that he retained complete confidence in her abilities. Two weeks later, the project coordinator resigned, leaving behind and unfinished an important project that she alone could complete.

The incident haunted this manager for weeks afterward, and he kept replaying in his mind the conversation she had initiated. But it wasn't until he learned about the belief system approach in the training session, he said, that he finally understood what he as a manager had done wrong.

When she came to me, she wasn't looking for a pep talk at all," he said he now realized. "She needed additional staffing to get her job done. She knew what the problem was, what was causing it, and how to solve it. All she really wanted was some help *from me* with the heavy work load. But I never asked her why she felt the way she did, or looked for the causes of the emotions that she was expressing. So she must have concluded that the situation was hopeless, and that was the reason why she left."

In wrapping up his story, this manager said regretfully, "If I had only thought to ask her why she felt the way she did, the cause of her problem would have come out, and we probably would have found a way to effectively solve it."

What Managers Rarely Do

This story illustrates what is perhaps the most important message for managers to draw from the belief system approach: Before trying to solve a motivation or performance problem, look for the causes of the problem first. And to find out what those causes are, go directly to the source—the person with the problem.

What this means is that communication is the key to motivation and performance improvement. Though this conclusion may seem obvious, rarely do managers think about it consciously and even more rarely do they put it into practice. If they did, a great many of the motivation and performance problems that plague today's business organizations would evaporate on the strength of surprisingly simple solutions.

In previous chapters we described how effective communication can be achieved through the belief system model and how it helped to facilitate change in a variety of industries with individuals, teams, and entire organizations. Our goal now is to describe these organizational applications in greater detail and show how the approach can be applied *systematically* in organizations that undertake large-scale change.

To do this, we'll present two case studies of organizations in transition: One involves the Human Resources department of an international corporation (see Chapter 8), the other involves a new sales organization within AT&T's Business Communications Services division (see Part IV). To identify, solve, and prevent the motivation and performance problems that were caused by change, both organizations used the four-part belief system process and the diagnostic tools that we'll describe; then each cascaded this process through multiple organizational levels.

PART I: TRAINING SESSIONS

Whenever we explain the belief system approach to managers, they invariably ask the same initial questions: How can we introduce the belief system into our organization? How do we get started?

Most managers recognize the importance of the approach almost immediately and readily understand the principles on which it's based. But since the belief system is unlike anything else in the management arena, figuring out how to implement it isn't always obvious. It's easy for managers to see, for example, how the one-on-one session can help to identify and solve motivation and performance problems. But how do they know which questions to ask, or how to ask them? How do they get employees to open up and talk about their deepest doubts and fears? And how do employees become convinced that they should accept responsibility for solving their own problems?

Clearly, both parties have to be carefully prepared for the one-on-one session, and this requires extensive training. In the two case studies that we'll describe, this training was delivered in a two-day session: the first day focusing on the background, principles, and objectives of the belief system approach; the second day focusing on the face-to-face meeting to come and how managers and employees can prepare for it.

What's unusual about the belief system training is that managers and their direct reports attend the training together. That's heresy in traditional training circles. "The boss of the trainees should never be present," the rationale goes, "because he or she will inhibit trainee responses." But we take a different position because we believe that there's no team when one or the other party is absent from the playing field. Employees cannot solve their own problems without the cooperation of their managers. And managers cannot solve motivation and performance problems without their employees' help.

PART II: ONE-ON-ONE SESSIONS

All the training that managers and employees receive in the belief system approach is targeted to ensuring the success of the critical interface called the one-on-one session. Usually lasting several hours, this meeting between managers and their direct reports is designed to accomplish two goals. One is to get employees involved in solving their own motivation and performance problems. The other is to improve the working relationship between managers and employees by helping them acquire a more informed understanding of each other.

The one-on-one session is the core of the belief system approach. When conducted effectively, it not only improves communication between managers and subordinates but also has the power to truly change things—and for the better. As an in-depth, investigatory process, the one-on-one session can achieve a variety of objectives:

- to identify or confirm what motivates the employee to perform well.

- to correct misperceptions or misunderstandings between managers and employees and remove barriers to effective performance.
- to identify and resolve existing motivation and performance problems.
- to bring potential motivation and performance problems to light and solve them.
- to improve communication between managers and employees and help them get to know each other better.

To ensure its effectiveness, the session is conducted as a supervised, facilitated meeting. The presence of an unbiased third party who's been trained in the belief system approach is critical in such an intimate discussion, where managers and employees often touch on personal and highly sensitive issues. But having a facilitator also helps to keep the session focused and on schedule, ensures that the conversation stays on track, and contributes substantially to achieving the session's objectives.

Manager and Employee Roles

While it is the manager who conducts the one-on-one session, the employee who participates is far from a passive player. The entire session, in fact, is designed as an employee-centered process. Everything that happens is founded on the proposition that employees should be equal partners with their managers when it comes to solving motivation and performance problems. This problem-solving methodology has proven highly effective for three simple reasons:

- Employees typically know more about their own performance problems than anyone else.
- Employees generally know what will solve their problems; that is, they know what will work for them.
- Employees have *preferred* ways of solving the problems they face, and when these solutions are carried out they usually work.

The one-on-one session is always conducted as a "structured" discussion—to maintain its problem-solving focus—but the way the session is carried out can vary, depending upon the work situation, how the participants have prepared for the meeting, and whether or not a performance problem exists or has yet to be identified. Nevertheless, the format of the session must always serve its ultimate purpose: to identify motivation and performance problems and come up with mutually acceptable solutions.

In essence, the one-on-one session is an overture that the manager extends to the employee to "help me to help you." The employee, of course, has the option to either help or refuse to cooperate. But in most cases the motivation to help is remarkably high because the employee is the first and most important beneficiary of this assistance.

The manager's primary role in the one-on-one session is to gather and share information. That means encouraging the employee to talk by asking specific and probing questions, then listening attentively to and interpreting what the employee says and reacting to it. The technique of paying close, unbiased attention to employee responses without interrupting is sometimes difficult for managers to master. But it can be done. And when it is, major breakthroughs in employee motivation often follow.

Four Diagnostic Tools

Conducting one-on-one sessions during change can be especially helpful because they allow managers to identify motivation and performance problems before they occur or prevent them from escalating. And they provide valuable opportunities for managers and employees to learn more about each other at a time when cooperation, communication, and teamwork are vitally important.

In the two case studies that we'll present, the organizations involved utilized four diagnostic tools as the basis for their one-on-one sessions. These tools are the Belief System Profile, Preferred Motivation Environment, Self-Diagnosis of Motivation/Performance Problem, and the Behavior Style Analysis. What follows is a brief description of each tool and how it can be used in the one-on-one session.

Belief System Profile

Designed as a written questionnaire in three parts, the Belief System Profile helps managers understand exactly what employees believe about their jobs: "Can I do it?" (B-1), "Will outcomes be tied to my performance?" (B-2), and "Will outcomes be satisfying?" (B-3). By providing accurate assessments of an employee's B-1, B-2, and B-3 beliefs, the Profile allows managers to pinpoint problems precisely and determine where to start improving on employee motivation and performance.

Each part of the Profile focuses on one of the three critical beliefs. Part I asks employees to make a list of the most important parts of their job, then indicate the degree of effort given to each task and the performance level normally achieved. The idea here is to get to the bottom of deep-seated B-1 confidence problems. (High effort and low performance, for example, indicate that a B-1 problem may exist.)

Part II of the Profile uncovers B-2 problems by asking employees to indicate how much they agree or disagree with a series of statements (e.g., "People who do a good job here are rewarded better than others"), while Part III focuses on the B-3 belief. It presents a long list of outcomes (Job Security, Money, Promotion, etc.) and then asks two questions: "How satisfying or dissatisfying would these outcomes be if you were to get them?" and "How much are you getting them?" The goal here is to determine whether (1) employees are not getting enough of what they want, or (2) employees are getting too much of what they don't want.

The Belief System Profile is filled out by the employee and the manager before the one-on-one session takes place (with the manager providing his or her perceptions of the employee's beliefs) and then they compare responses when they meet face to face.

Preferred Motivation Environment

The objective of this tool is to identify what truly motivates the employee and to determine what kind of work environment would match his or her personal preferences as closely as possible. For example, some employees enjoy a fast-paced, ever-changing work environment, while others prefer jobs that are characterized by harmony, predictability, and routine.

To uncover this information, the Preferred Motivation Environment asks the employee a series of questions that become progressively more sensitive and require increasingly more disclosure. Some questions are designed to identify the good things the manager does that motivates the employee, as well as the bad things that inhibit motivation and performance, and they explore what the manager might do differently to create a more motivating work environment. Other questions prompt the employee to reveal his or her most private job-related fears and insecurities, so that the manager truly understands the person that he or she is trying to accommodate.

The information gleaned from the Preferred Motivation Environment can serve as the basis for a productive one-on-one session and provide a wealth of valuable insights for managers on how to motivate employees to perform better.

Preferred Motivation Environment (sample questions)

What are the things your manager sometimes says or does that may hold back your motivation and performance?

When you do a good job, does your manager generally acknowledge it in an appropriate way?

Of all the things you would like your manager to know about you, which ones are you most reluctant to discuss?

Self-Diagnosis of Motivation/Performance Problem

This tool allows employees to diagnose motivation and performance problems on their own, before the one-on-one session takes place. Though their manager may suggest a problem for them to diagnose, employees may revise the problem identified by their manager or recommend a different problem altogether.

Following the Self-Diagnosis worksheets, employees are asked to determine the type of work problem they're experiencing (B-1, B-2, or B-3), to identify possible causes of the problem and to come up with workable solutions. With this information in hand, they can then walk into the one-on-one session well prepared to solve at least one problem that the manager knows about, and may bring up other motivation and performance problems that their manager is unaware of.

While it is the employee who fills out the Self-Diagnosis, the manager uses a similar form (called the Best-Guess Diagnosis) that prompts him or her to evaluate the employee's problem *from the employee's point of view*. Then later, during the one-on-one session, employee and manager can compare their diagnoses. Sometimes they're similar; many times they're not. But closing the gaps in perception and understanding and getting the employee involved in solving his or her own problems is what results.

Self-Diagnosis of Motivation/Performance (sample questions)

If your manager does not have a complete and accurate perception of your performance, what evidence can you give to correct any misunderstandings?

Will you be able to meet performance expectations if your proposed solutions are approved?

What will it take to persuade your manager to support the solutions you prefer?

Behavior Style Analysis

This is one of the most helpful tools used by organizations that implement the belief system approach. Designed as a twenty-four-item questionnaire, the Behavior Style Analysis is based on the model of behavior developed by William Moulton Marston and John Geier. When used as the basis for a one-on-one discussion, it can provide valuable insights into B-3 beliefs (i.e., what's satisfying and what's dissatisfying to the person) and can help employees and their managers gain a better understanding of each other's personality and work style.

The tool is based on research showing that people demonstrate four basic behavior styles:

- *Dominant Behavior Style (High-D):* People with a dominant behavior style tend to be aggressive, authoritarian, decisive, and bottom-line oriented. Impatient, with strong egos, they will charge ahead with only a small amount of information and are not highly receptive to suggestions from others.
- *Influencing Behavior Style (High-I):* People with this style tend to be persuasive, convincing, charming, and always ready with a quip or a solution. At ease among strangers, they are sometimes impulsive, are poorly suited to detail work, and make excellent point men or women.
- *Steady Behavior Style (High-S):* Quintessential team players, High-S people are steady and reliable, though usually unspectacular, and are always there when you need them. They're not prone to initiate change, complain, or clash with anyone; they carry out the program, maintain the status quo, and protect and "mother" their brood.
- *Cautious Behavior Style (High-C):* People with this style tend to follow the well-beaten path and are not inclined to stray into new or unfamiliar territory. Highly detail oriented, they're a great counterbalance to High-D and High-I people. Though they sometimes lose sight of the big picture, they never miss anything in the small print.

Behavior Style Analysis (sample characteristics)

High-D	High-I	High-S	High-C
Likes change	Talkative	Patient	Accurate
Intimidating	Articulate	Relaxed	Cautious
Risk taker	Creative	Supportive	Risk averse
Positive	Poised	Controlled	Sensitive
Problem solver	Persuasive	Dependable	Detailed
Not a good listener	Makes a good impression	Difficulty prioritizing	Complies with authority

According to this model, most people have both a *primary* and a *secondary* behavior style. A High-D person may exhibit many "I" tendencies, for example, and High-S's often exhibit many characteristics of the "C" behavior style. No style is good or bad; each has its strengths and weaknesses, and no one style is better than the others.

Understanding behavior styles, however, can be helpful in dealing with people and in developing good work relationships. After all, the more you know about someone, the easier it is to get along with that person on the job. You can predict how he or she will react in certain situations, communicate better, and accomplish more together. Behavior style information is especially valuable to managers, who can boost the performance of their subordinates simply by putting them in work situations that are suited to their behavioral tendencies.

Behavior style can also provide the basis for productive discussions during one-on-one sessions. When both manager and employee know each other's behavior style, they can each talk about the aspects of the other person's style that they most appreciate, which motivation and performance problems are caused by behavioral tendencies, and what changes can be made to develop a more harmonious and effective working relationship. Then they can each make a list of commitments to implement those changes. The value of this exercise is threefold:

- Manager and employee gain a better understanding and appreciation of each other—no small gain when it comes to team performance.
- Manager and employee get along better by developing ways to accommodate each other's style.
- Manager and employee learn to work better as a team by making a list of commitments that they both agree will bring about improvement in performance.

The Four Diagnostic Tools

Belief System Profile—corrects misperceptions the manager may harbor about the employee's motivation and removes barriers to performance.

Preferred Motivation Environment—identifies those things that motivate the employee to perform well and makes those findings known to the manager.

Self-Diagnosis of Motivation/Performance Problem—identifies employee performance problems and, in concert with the manager, solves them.

Behavior Style Analysis—promotes better working relationships between managers and employees by helping them to develop an understanding and appreciation of each other's behavior tendencies.

Conducting the One-on-One

In the belief system approach, the one-on-one session is where the "rubber meets the road." It is from this exchange between manager and employee that motivation and performance problems surface and their solutions materialize. Both problems and solutions reside in the employee, but he or she can do little to bring about improvement without the manager's intervention. Until the manager creates the right environment for the problem and solution to emerge, they lie dormant within the employee, waiting to be discovered. The one-on-one session is the vehicle managers use to gently coax these problems and solutions from the employee and bring them to light.

During the one-on-one session, managers should ask probing questions and listen carefully to what the employee has to say, for in those responses will lie important clues about the problems that need to be solved. Another tip: Don't allow emotional outbursts to derail the one-on-one session or sidetrack the discussion. Instead, when strong emotions surface (and they often do during these sessions), confront them directly. They can provide important clues that tell you where problems lie, how serious they are, and what may be causing them. By asking the single question, "Why do you feel the way you do?" managers may uncover a wealth of valuable information that can be critical to the success of the session.

When an employee's problem is diagnosed, the manager should summarize it clearly for the employee and ask for any corrections or additions. This summary should be a brief restatement of the B-1, B-2, and B-3 problem, including any causes mentioned by the employee. Nothing else is required at this time. There's no need for any explanations or justifications, criticism or sympathy, lectures or finger pointing. The manager should simply state the diagnosis and then wait for the employee's feedback to make sure the summary of the problem is correct. Here's an example:

Manager: So what you're saying is that even if you work hard, you can't do the kind of job you want to do because you don't fully understand all the new procedures. [The employee is saying, "I can't do it." The cause is the new procedures.]

Employee: You've hit it right on the head. [Now the manager knows that the employee has a B-1 problem and also knows the cause of it.]

When manager and employee agree on the problem and its causes, the manager is uniquely prepared to guide the employee toward finding solutions. This begins when the manager asks the employee for solutions. There's no intent to curry favor here. Making employees feel good is important but secondary to a higher objective: finding effective solutions to real problems. So managers should resist the temptation to offer their suggestions, and let the employee come up with his or her own solutions.

Some employees will be eager to say what they think; others won't. But employees always have ideas about how to solve their problems, so the manager should be encouraging and keep asking until the message is clear: "I would like and value your ideas for solving the problem." To draw the employee out, the manager can try statements like, "What do you think is the best way to handle this?" or "I really would be interested in what you think we should do."

The manager should summarize the employee's suggestions to make sure that he or she understands the key points of what the employee is saying. It's a fatal mistake to seek out solutions and then move ahead with a misunderstanding of what the employee said. Summarizing is the best check against that happening.

Sometimes the solution recommended by the employee will be satisfactory, and the manager can move on. But when the solution isn't acceptable, the manager should pose questions that help the employee see the wisdom of an alternative solution:

Manager: Let me get this straight. You want to start work at 6:30 and finish the day by 2:30? What are you going to do about engineering support? Bob doesn't come in until 8:45.

Employee: Oh, I see what you mean. I guess flextime isn't going to work in this case.

If the employee continues to offer solutions that are inappropriate or farfetched, the manager should

- Ask questions about the solutions that reveal the difficulties in adopting them ("How would you go about implementing this?").
- Point out flaws in the solutions and offer suggestions for overcoming them.
- Keep asking for additional ideas until a solution surfaces that both manager and employee can agree to.

Once agreement has been reached on the best solution to the problem, both parties must make a commitment—the employee to solve the problem, the manager to help the employee. Here's the procedure: First the manager summarizes the solution they've agreed to. Then the employee commits to implementing it. The summary should include both what the employee has to do and what the manager commits to do:

Manager: Let me see if I've got this right. You want to meet with Bob two or three times for an hour or so each time?

Employee: That should do it.

Manager: Do you think this will get your performance up to where it should be?

Employee: Yes, I think it will solve the problem. I'll certainly dig in to make it work. [This is the employee's commitment.]

Manager: O.K. I'll talk with Bob and have him get in touch with you to set up a time for the first meeting. [This is the manager's commitment.]

When the one-on-one session is completed and all issues have been addressed and resolved, the manager should end the discussion on a positive note. To do this, the manager should

- Thank the employee for participating in the session.
- Express appreciation for the employee's willingness to talk openly and honestly.
- Offer ongoing help and agree to conduct follow-up discussions, if needed, to ensure success in solving the problem.

PART III: TEAM MEETING

The main objective of the one-on-one session is to come up with mutually agreeable solutions and commitments to get problems corrected. Based on this agreement, both manager and employee write on their respective To Do lists those things that they have committed to carry out to solve identified problems. Productive change is the goal: change from old ways that inhibited motivation and performance to new ways that unleash the power of unfettered joint action.

To ensure that these commitments are kept, it often helps to hold a team meeting after a manager has met one on one with his or her direct reports. Guided by a trained facilitator, this session allows managers and employees to identify common themes that surfaced during the one-on-one sessions and to confirm any new approaches or solutions that have been proposed.

The team meeting is especially beneficial to the manager, because different employees on a team often suffer from similar problems and voice similar concerns. It's not uncommon, in fact, for managers to hear the same comments during their one-on-one sessions with employees: "Your performance expectations are unrealistic," "You don't provide enough direction on assignments," or "You don't spend enough time with us." Highlighting and discussing these common themes can provide the manager with guidelines for setting a new course of action or prompt a much-needed change in management style.

PART IV: FOLLOW-UP SESSIONS

Establishing commitments on both sides to change and take action is not the end of the belief system process, however. How will the efforts to solve problems be monitored? And what kind of follow-up must be done by both the manager and the employee to make sure the commitments become realities?

Conducting a follow-up one-on-one session, usually about six months after the initial meeting, allows both manager and employee to review their written commitments, determine what progress has been made in solving motivation and performance problems, and decide whether additional steps must be taken. If necessary, both parties can amend their To Do lists at this time to reflect the progress they've achieved and outline a new course of action to resolve ongoing concerns.

The one-on-one follow-up sessions are also vital to keeping the belief system alive and ensure that the approach becomes an established practice in an organization. When they are conducted on a regular basis, they play a critical role in preventing new motivation and performance problems and ensuring that old ones don't recur.

Four-Part Belief System Process

Part I: Training Sessions

Part II: One-on-One Sessions

Part III: Team Meeting

Part IV: Follow-Up Sessions

IMPLEMENTING THE MODEL AT MULTIPLE LEVELS

We believe that the four-part belief system process that we described is the best way for managers to implement the belief system change model. To maximize the benefits of its practices and tools, some managers apply it organizationwide through a systematic process that we call "cascading."

Cascading is the implementation of the belief system approach at multiple organizational levels. This can be done consecutively, first at the highest level and then on each organizational level below it, or simultaneously, at more than one organizational level at the same time. In either case, the objective is the same: to ensure that everyone in the organization participates with his or her manager in a one-on-one session and has the opportunity to resolve change-related motivation and performance problems.

Cascading is not an integral component of the belief system approach: individual managers can apply the model on their own, within their departments or with their teams. But cascading is recommended whenever an organization undergoes change on a large scale or implements change initiatives companywide. In short, when the impact of change is felt by everyone in your organization, cascading the belief system is one of the best strategies you can use to help your people cope and deal with change.

In the remaining chapters of this book, we'll describe how the belief system change model was cascaded in two large business organizations and report the benefits and results they achieved from implementing this approach from top to bottom.

8

Managing Change from Top to Bottom: A Case Study of Large-Scale Change

In a business book published several years ago, two management experts attempted to answer the critical question, "Why do so many change efforts fail?" The conclusion they came to was that the lack of success cannot be attributed to weak change leadership. Most managers are willing to define ambitious new goals for their organization and create business strategies to achieve them. But far fewer are aware of the need for effective change management and can successfully guide their organization through the transition process.

"Many strategic plans die because of lack of implementation," these experts explained. "There is a high correlation between the failure to implement changes and the lack of conscious management of the transitional process."[1] Why do managers focus more on leading than managing change? One reason is that the latter is more people intensive and harder to do. It involves effectively communicating the change strategy, building awareness and commitment to new goals, and maintaining high levels of motivation and performance throughout the transition process.

Though many managers see these as relatively minor issues during change, they are in fact the most common stumbling blocks to implementing change successfully and should be considered management priorities. As these experts concluded, "In an effective change effort—particularly when a fundamental change is required—it is critical for top management to pay attention to the process of change and transition, in addition to leading the change itself."[2]

Organizational Upheaval

In the case study we are about to describe, these issues were not neglected or minimized. On the contrary, the leaders of this organization recognized the importance of managing change and of helping their people to adjust and cope with transition. By implementing the belief system approach at every level, they helped their organization to successfully make it through a difficult period of change, and it reemerged as strong as before—and in some ways stronger than ever.

This was no small feat considering the scope and magnitude of the changes that this organization went through. A large Human Resources department within a multinational corporation, it was downsized from over 900 employees to about 300 at a time when nearly 100 thousand people were laid off companywide. Operating as a profit center and competing against outside suppliers for internal customers, it had to rethink its entire operation and change the processes it had used for providing HR services, such as recruitment, selection and evaluation, training and development, and personnel record keeping.

Not only was the impact of the downsizing devastating to morale, the changes it required were also wreaking havoc with many employees. Fewer people had to accomplish more work, managers had less time to spend with their direct reports, frazzled employees had to learn new procedures, and the intensified pressure to perform put everyone out of sorts. Each employee had to pull his or her weight—and then some—and the prospect of profitability looked increasingly unachievable.

Emotions Run Amok

Following the downsizing, the emotional climate within the organization changed dramatically, and for the worse. Fear was the predominant and most unsettling feeling among employees: No matter how many times they were told that the downsizing was over, many continued to believe that additional personnel cuts would take place and that they would eventually lose their jobs.

Anger was another strong emotion that pervaded the entire organization. Not only were people hostile to the planned changes, they were infuriated with management for terminating longtime coworkers and friends, and they resented having to take on additional work responsibilities with fewer resources and less support.

These job changes also triggered intense feelings of anxiety and inadequacy. To achieve greater efficiencies, new methods and procedures had to be developed to replace established work practices, but this meant that some people had to learn their job all over again or master an entirely new position. "Not only has my work load increased substantially," people would complain, "but now I've got to do things I've never done before."

CASCADING THE CHANGE MODEL

During this period of disruption and discontent, the belief system of motivation and performance was implemented at the highest management levels within the organization and then cascaded down to the lowest ranks. Nearly 300 people in all participated in the process that included training sessions, one-on-one sessions, team meetings, and follow-up sessions. (For a detailed description of the four-part belief system process, see Chapter 7.)

The decision to introduce the belief system was made by the organization's top-ranking executive, the Vice President of Human Resources. A no-nonsense, bottom-line-oriented manager, this executive had laid his career on the line with a bold forecast of profitability that he could not possibly deliver unless his people performed as never before. But having seen the belief system in action and convinced of its validity, he believed that this new approach to managing change could ignite motivation and performance in his organization and help his people to survive and succeed at change.

In January 1992, it was this executive's team, consisting of eight department heads, that was the first in the organization to undergo training in the belief system approach. One-on-one sessions were conducted with team members throughout March and April, and a team meeting was conducted in May. The following February, in 1993, follow-up one-on-one sessions were held for all executive team members.

Cascade Timetable

January 1992: Two-day training session conducted with
    executive team

March–April 1992: One-on-one sessions conducted for
    executive team

May 1992: Team meeting conducted for executive team

September 1992–December 1993: Belief system process
    cascaded throughout the 300-member organization

February 1993: Follow-up one-on-one sessions conducted
    with executive team

Cascading the belief system approach throughout the organization began in September 1992 and proceeded through December 1993. To prepare for their one-on-one sessions, which were facilitated by employees who received special training in the belief system approach, both managers and their direct reports used the four diagnostic tools that were described in Chapter 7: the Belief System Profile, Preferred Motivation Environment, Self-Diagnosis of Motivation/Performance Problem, and the Behavior Style Analysis.

Resistance and Acceptance

At first, not all employees in the organization were receptive to the belief system approach. Some, in fact, reacted with hostility when they were told about the one-on-one session that they would have to participate in with their manager. In the wake of the downsizing, this response was understandable. Many people in the organization were feeling strong negative emotions following the layoffs, and they were uncomfortable with the idea of opening up and talking frankly with their managers.

Some employees also resented having to lose valuable work time because they were required to attend training sessions and one-on-one interviews. "First you double my work load," employees would complain. "Now you make me waste my day sitting in a conference room to learn an improvement process that I've never heard about before."

Yet once the one-on-one sessions got underway, positive word-of-mouth quickly began to change employee attitudes. When people heard about the effectiveness of the approach in solving problems—and how good their coworkers felt after their one-on-one sessions—they became less apprehensive about participating and even began to look forward to meeting with their managers.

Most of these sessions were highly productive because the changes the organization was going through had generated a wealth of motivation and performance problems. B-1 issues were widespread, for example, due to the increase in workloads and the introduction of new procedures. "Can I really handle this?" was the question that many employees were asking themselves, or "Do I have the right skills to meet the higher expectations that have been set for my job?"

B-2 problems were also prevalent because raises and promotions were no longer readily available, and people began to question whether they would get the kind of compensation that they truly deserved. "With all these cutbacks and cost-cutting measures," many people were thinking, "will I be rewarded the way I should be, even if I work hard and do a good job?"

The radical changes that took place, the increased pressure to perform, and the everyday stress of change all contributed to a growing dissatisfaction with working in the organization, prompting serious B-3 problems. Many people began to ponder the questions, "Do I really want to continue working here under these conditions?" and "Will I ever enjoy my work again, even when I get used to my new job?"

Steady Improvement

In the six months after the belief system was introduced, the Vice President of Human Resources noticed a marked improvement in both organizational morale and performance. Bottom-line results were substantially stronger, and the benefits of the approach seemed to grow the lower the levels it reached. Since most of the real work was done there, the entire organization seemed to be floating higher in the water.

Team effectiveness also improved significantly, not just up and down the chain of command, but horizontally as well. And because managers and their direct reports were beginning to understand each other better, conflicts—both real and potential—were able to be resolved at lower levels, before they became entrenched.

This development was especially pleasing to the Vice President, because problems that used to find their way to his desk for resolution—frequently after things had gone too far to be salvaged—no longer came his way. Now he had the time to devote to other, more pressing issues, and his people could spend more of their time tending to business.

Eventually, the belief system became such an accepted approach in the organization for preventing and resolving problems that people began to use it in innovative ways, outside the four-part process. Every month, for example, the Vice President would regularly conduct two consecutive days of meetings with his executive team. He decided to incorporate the belief system into the team's decision-making processes, adopting the language of the approach and applying its method for diagnosing problems.

If team members were debating whether or not to introduce a new HR service, for instance, they would ask, "What potential B-1 problems could this create in our organization?" Then they'd follow up with the questions, "Who would be most affected by these problems?" and "What would we have to do to prevent or minimize them?" Using the belief system in this way helped the team make more effective decisions for the organization and reinforced the value of the approach among its members, making it easier for them to bring about continued improvements with their own teams.

Others began to utilize parts of the belief system process as tools for team building. Each member of a team, for example, would exchange the results of his or her Behavior Style Analysis with other members, thus sharing important information about personality and working style. In this way, team members would learn about each other's preferred ways of communicating, solving problems, and making decisions, which helped reduce conflict on teams and increased their effectiveness.

PROFILES OF INDIVIDUAL CHANGE

As the belief system was cascaded throughout the organization, numerous anecdotes and stories emerged about how the approach was helping to resolve change-related problems, improve working relationships, and boost the performance of both teams and individuals. One story concerned the head of the organization, the Vice President of Human Resources, and how the one-on-one sessions he conducted with his team prompted him to modify his management style and increased his awareness of the impact he had on his people.

An aggressive high achiever with little patience for indecision (a typical High-D according to his Behavior Style Analysis), this executive tended to treat all his subordinates virtually the same way (for a description of the four behavior styles, see Chapter 7). He was abrupt and direct with them—even confrontational when he felt it was necessary—and wasted no time on small talk or details. A seasoned business professional, he assumed that his working style produced the best results and that it was the most effective way to manage his people.

During the one-on-one sessions with his team, however, this executive learned that instead of appreciating his authoritative leadership the people he managed often found it annoying and demotivating. His style was not always "in sync" with theirs, he discovered, and his inflexibility was undermining his team's effectiveness. Several common themes surfaced in these discussions:

- *Lack of clear expectations.* True to his personality style, the Vice President tended to issue broad-brush directives regarding organizational change, without going into detail about how they should be carried out. Some of his subordinates saw this as a lack of clear expectations. Because they didn't know exactly what the Vice President wanted, they felt they couldn't perform well and began to develop B-1 problems, marked by feelings of inadequacy and low confidence.
- *Impatience and unwillingness to listen.* On those occasions when they asked the Vice President for help, many members of the executive team simply wanted to talk through their problems and come up with solutions on their

own. But the Vice President, impatient to charge ahead and get things done quickly, would jump in and solve their problems for them. Instead of listening attentively, he would mandate his own solutions and ignore the suggestions that his subordinates would propose.

• *Not managing to the individual.* Perhaps the most important message the Vice President received from these sessions was that he treated all his subordinates the same and was not managing to the individuality of each team member. While some team members admired him for his commanding and aggressive style, most of them disliked being treated in this way and wanted to be managed in a way that they preferred.

For the Vice President, these sessions represented a crucial turning point in establishing work relationships that would become more enjoyable and more productive. In the past, he had never bothered to meet with team members individually to explore their problems and concerns. But now, with an in-depth understanding of each member's style and how they wanted to be managed, he felt he had the critical information he needed to improve team performance during the change and maintain the motivation that was required for success.

Transforming Work Relationships

Similar stories of individual change and transformation came from every organizational level as the belief system was implemented from top to bottom in the Human Resources organization. One story involved an accountant in the finance department, whose personality and work style differed sharply from those of her manager.

A High-C according to her Behavior Style Analysis, this woman was a consummate professional whose perfectionist tendencies worked against her during this time of major transition. Though her workload had increased substantially, she refused to compromise her standards and became increasingly bogged down in her duties. Loath to delegate important tasks to her subordinates, she assumed more and more responsibility and worked later into the night, yet she stilled missed critical deadlines and started to feel overwhelmed and ineffective.

Whenever this accountant scheduled a meeting with her boss, she always arrived with piles of computer printouts and reports and an itemized agenda of what she felt they needed to discuss. But her manager, a High-D with little tolerance for financial minutiae, would consistently find an excuse to cut their meeting short and usher her quickly out of the office. "I've spent all this time trying to accomplish what needs to get done," she would say to herself, "and my boss doesn't even recognize my efforts. What's the point of doing this job right if no one really appreciates it?"

By the time this accountant was scheduled to meet with her manager for their one-on-one session, the tension between them was palpable and both expected a head-on confrontation. But after a slow start, they soon realized that they could each make adjustments in work style that would satisfy the other. After a long conversation about their different personalities and job expectations, they then settled into a friendly discussion about how each could change to improve their relationship.

In the end, the accountant agreed to focus on compiling only those reports that the organization really needed—and not feel obligated to present her boss with a certified financial statement every month—and to avoid spending hours checking and rechecking her data. In return, her manager agreed to be more patient with her during their meetings, to acknowledge her efforts more, and not withhold the recognition that was needed to maintain her motivation. In only a short time, as each worked to fulfill these commitments, the accountant's confidence and performance began to improve, and she and her manager developed a more comfortable and satisfying relationship.

Increasing Awareness and Understanding

In many organizations that implement the belief system approach, much of the improvement that occurs can be attributed to an increase in mutual understanding between managers and subordinates and to a better awareness of each other's needs and preferences. There are two stories from our case study that demonstrate how the belief system helps to make this happen and how it encourages the kind of communication that can dramatically change work relationships.

One involved a low-level technician in the organization's finance department. This woman, who was over sixty and approaching retirement, was a dedicated worker and proficient at her job. But every time her boss asked her to do something out of the ordinary—a request that became frequent during the change effort—she nearly always resisted. Though she'd accept each assignment and never argued with her boss, she'd typically procrastinate on those projects that required her to perform functions she was unfamiliar with, and many assignments would never be completed. Eventually, her boss became fed up with her and began to think about hiring a replacement.

When this issue came up in their one-on-one session, the technician was reluctant at first to admit that she even had a performance problem or that her manager had reason to feel frustrated with her behavior. But as the conversation progressed and she began to open up, she made an emotional disclosure that cast a new light on the problem, and it led to a workable solution.

Throughout her childhood, she related almost in tears, her mother habitually discouraged her from venturing out on her own or trying anything different. As a consequence, she became comfortable only with routine as an adult and would freeze up emotionally whenever she was asked to do something new. "All my life, my mother has told me, 'You can't do that,'" the technician revealed during the session. And those maternal warnings, she said, still echoed in her head.

When the technician's manager heard this story, he began to think about what he could do to rectify the situation, and he offered this suggestion. "In the future," he proposed to her, "whenever I ask you to do something that you've never done before, let's sit down and talk about it before-hand, and I'll walk you through the project step by step. I promise not to throw a new assignment on your desk and just walk out the door. If you have questions about what you should do, feel free to come to me for help, and I'll try to provide you with any assistance that you need."

Reassured by his understanding and offer of support, the technician eventually became more comfortable when tackling new assignments and, buoyed by a renewed feeling of self-confidence, she continued to work for the same boss for several years to come.

Providing Direction and Guidance

A similar story had to do with a high-ranking manager whose relationship with his boss deteriorated considerably when their organization began to change. Like the technician we just described, he felt he needed more direction and guidance from his boss and that the lack of support was undermining his effectiveness. But until he participated in their one-on-one session, this manager never told his boss how he felt and just continued to suffer in silence.

The night before the session was to take place, the manager called up the belief system facilitator and, in a trembling voice, asked him to come over for a private meeting right away. When the facilitator arrived, the manager seemed agitated and upset, and he made a surprise announcement: He had decided to submit his resignation to his boss during the one-on-one session on the following day. "The performance of my group isn't good, and I can't seem to turn it around," he explained. "And a big part of the problem is that my boss won't tell me what to do. He sets all these goals for me and then just sends me off to figure things out for myself. But I'm the kind of person who needs structure and guidance. If I'm given a goal, I want some direction on how to get there."

After calming this manager down, the facilitator asked him to put off his decision to resign, at least until after the one-on-one session.

Then he advised him, "During your meeting tomorrow, tell your boss exactly what you've told me, and see if the two of you can work this problem out." Although the manager was skeptical that a satisfactory solution could be reached, he agreed to tell his boss what was on his mind and to put his faith in the belief system approach.

When this manager left his one-on-one session the following day, he felt as if he had a new life ahead of him, he told the facilitator. Not only had his boss listened carefully to his concerns during the meeting, he apologized for neglecting to provide enough direction and pledged to develop a new working relationship with the manager. In the future, this boss wrote on his To Do list, he would allot more time to clarifying expectations, providing direction, and helping the manager with follow-through and implementation—and not expect results simply by issuing orders.

GAUGING THE SUCCESS OF THE CHANGE

A year after the belief system was introduced into this organization, a number of quantitative indicators pointed to the effectiveness of the approach. For the Vice President of Human Resources, the most significant of these were the measures that showed a substantial improvement in bottom-line results. Revenues for the year, he noted, had surpassed the aggressive goal he set the year before by 20 percent, while expenses rose only 8 percent. Profit as a percent of revenue rose to an impressive 10 percent, also exceeding his forecast.

Employee Opinions

Several surveys administered at this time also helped the organization to weigh the impact of the belief system approach. One was a leadership questionnaire that asked employees to respond to eighteen statements that described their relationship with their boss and how it changed through the belief system process. After each statement, employees were asked to evaluate their manager by circling either "strongly disagree," "disagree," "agree," or "strongly agree."

The data from this survey showed, as a result of the belief system training and application, employees felt as follows:

At least 80 percent of employees "agreed" or "strongly agreed," when presented with the following statements:

- My manager understands me better (95%).
- My manager adapts more to my style (93%).
- My manager and I communicate better (90%).

- My manager makes better decisions about me (88%).
- My manager is more effective with me (88%).
- My manager has more respect for me (85%).
- My manager and I have a better relationship (83%).
- My manager and I are more open and honest with each other (83%).
- My manager and I work together better (83%).
- It is safer to say what I think to my manager (80%).
- This is a better place to work (80%).

At least 60 percent of employees "agreed" or "strongly agreed" with these statements:

- My manager treats me better (78%).
- The belief system has been well worth the time I have invested in it (75%).
- I am performing better (65%).
- I like my job better (63%).

At least 45 percent of employees "agreed" or "strongly agreed" with the following statements:

- I am more motivated (53%).
- I am more confident in my future (48%).
- The belief system has been a breakthrough experience for me (45%).

Measuring Added Value

But how did these opinions translate into value for the organization, a measure that the Vice President put great stock in? How did the belief system add value for its employees? How did the belief system add value for its customers?

Some answers came from the results of the organization's annual employee survey. Data from this lengthy questionnaire, which allowed employees to express their views on sixteen categories of questions covering a wide range of corporate issues, pointed to high levels of employee satisfaction—dramatically improved over the year prior to introducing the belief system and even higher than those for the company as a whole. While a 65-percent approval rating is considered remarkably high in any employee survey, these results showed that

- at least 70 percent of employees responded favorably in five of the sixteen categories of questions (up from 1 in 15 categories before the belief system).

- 65 to 69 percent responded favorably in six other categories of questions (up from 4 in 15 categories before the belief system).
- 60 to 64 responded favorably in two categories of questions (same as 2 in 15 categories before the belief system).
- 50 to 59 percent responded favorably to 2 categories of questions (down from 5 in fifteen categories before the belief system).
- 30 to 49 percent responded favorably in the one remaining category of questions (down from 3 of 15 categories before the belief system).

A comparison of these results to those for the entire company showed that

- approval ratings from Human Resource employees exceeded those for the company as a whole in all sixteen categories.
- in eight of the sixteen categories, approval ratings from Human Resource employees exceeded those for the company by at least 10 percentage points.

A separate survey conducted among the organization's customers also reflected favorably on the belief system approach. In this survey, some 95 percent of the respondents said that they were "satisfied, very satisfied, or delighted" with the products and services provided by the human resources organization; some 55 percent said that they were "delighted."

These results, and the many stories of improved motivation and performance that emerged during the implementation, show that the belief system was worthwhile and paid off handsomely for this organization. In part IV, we'll present another case study of how the belief system helped to manage large-scale change. Once again, we'll present both quantitative and qualitative data to gauge the effectiveness of the approach.

NOTES

1. See Richard Beckard and Wendy Pritchard, *Changing the Essence: The Art of Creating and Leading Fundamental Change in Organizations* (San Francisco: Jossey-Bass, 1992), 69.

2. Ibid., 92.

_____ PART IV

THE BCS/MIDDLE MARKETS STORY

9

The Setting for Change

Too many of the business books and articles that deal with change these days focus only on the success stories. In their efforts to outline an easy-to-follow recipe for renewal, these writings neglect to analyze the many companies that collapse during change or get swallowed up in the confusion and chaos that typically follow it. This oversight may explain why some people fail to understand the risks that are involved with change and the impact that change can have on human lives. Many don't realize that in most change efforts the potential for failure is high and the emotional and psychological repercussions can be immense.

Even those of us who have been through a major change effort find it hard to accurately convey the emotional intensity of the experience and all the fears and apprehensions that go with it. To give others some idea of what this was like at the BCS division of AT&T, the case study that we are about to describe, the story of the sixteenth-century Spanish conquistador Hernando Cortez and his enemy, Montezuma, may prove illuminating.

Arriving in the New World with only 400 troops, Cortez was vastly outnumbered when he mounted his assault against the famous Aztec leader, whose experienced and well-disciplined army totaled more than eight thousand. To steel his soldiers for the confrontation that lay ahead—and eliminate any thoughts of turning around and sailing back to Spain—Cortez took drastic steps: He ordered the burning of the three ships that he and his army had arrived on, and then told his men that they had no choice but to prepare for battle and forge ahead.

If you can imagine the thoughts and feelings of those soldiers, you have some idea of what people were experiencing when the effort to create a new sales organization within BCS began at the end of 1994: fear mixed with excitement, anxiety compounded by confusion, and an overwhelming desire to turn back the clock. "When I try to remember what I was thinking at the time we started Middle Markets, it's all a big blur now," one BCS manager told us. "It was unsettling at first— I felt scared and anxious—but there was also a tremendous feeling of empowerment."

Though the battle being waged by BCS was not the life-and-death struggle that Cortez and his men faced, BCS employees nevertheless knew that the business stakes involved with the startup of Middle Markets were substantial and there was no guarantee of success. What's more, despite the many changes that had taken place in AT&T since the breakup of 1984, what BCS was trying to do was unprecedented in the company—a true "frontier experience," as one of its managers put it. In essence, BCS was heading into unknown territory without backup, and had no way of knowing beforehand all the problems it would encounter, especially the emotional obstacles that the change effort would involve.

Signs of Emotional Upheaval

Complicating this situation was the fact that by the early 1990s the telecommunications industry was by any measure one of the most competitive in the United States. This meant that any additional pressures placed on BCS employees in creating a new sales organization would push them to stress levels that could have potentially dangerous consequences. Though no one could predict the specific emotional responses the change effort would provoke, there were suspicions that the situation was perilously close to the limit of what employees could be reasonably expected to endure.

Though many change leaders come to this realization only with hindsight, there are usually signs along the way that indicate the emotional toll that change is taking. Among them are shorter tempers, more frequent emotional outbursts, and misplaced anger and frustration (kick-the-dog syndrome). In the case of BCS, extreme behaviors like these became more prevalent in the last quarter of 1994, during the transition to Middle Markets, when many recruits to the new organization were still performing their previous job while trying to learn their new one.

Behavioral Indicators of the Emotional Impact of Change

- Short tempers
- Angry outbursts
- Tearful exchanges
- Kick-the-dog syndrome
- Excessive aggressiveness
- Temperamental flare-ups
- Outward displays of negativity
- Increased absenteeism
- Declining performance

In interviews conducted much later in the change effort, the feelings behind these behaviors were openly discussed. "The launch of Middle Markets was a terrible time for me personally," one manager confided. "I felt like I was doing two jobs at the same time, and the workloads and long hours were a problem." Said another manager, "I was excited about the change and felt that we got a lot of support. But I was constantly tired and stressed out at the time, and the transition from my old accounts was a tough one to make."

Though emotional responses to changes like these are not uncommon, few organizations recognize the importance of working through them, or they adopt a head-in-the-sand approach whenever strong emotions begin to surface. At BCS, the response was different. Aware of the high stress levels that were already part of their culture, management had a basic understanding that structural change alone was not sufficient to accomplish the organization's new objectives and that something more was needed to help people cope with major change. For that reason, the decision was taken by senior management in late 1994 to introduce the belief system approach and to cascade it throughout the Eastern Region of Middle Markets.

CUSTOMER-DRIVEN ORGANIZATIONAL CHANGE

Why was change necessary within BCS? Like many other business organizations that undertake major change today, two overriding factors were having a significant impact on the strategic direction BCS was taking: changes in its customers and increased competition.

The business of BCS is to provide companies of all sizes with a variety of telecommunications services, ranging from long-distance calling to sophisticated global data networks. Though the percentage of all U.S. businesses that purchase these services from AT&T has historically been high, BCS began to lose significant market share in the late 1980s to a growing number of strong competitors, and in 1993 undertook a comprehensive study to determine why.

In analyzing the buying behaviors of various types of business organizations, what BCS found out through research confirmed what some of its managers had long suspected: AT&T was underserving a significant and growing portion of business customers—those known as "mid-size" companies. These overlooked customers included high-growth, entrepreneurial firms—many of them startups in the economic boom of the 1980s—that had annual sales revenues of between $20 million and $250 million and employed anywhere from 25 to 500 people.

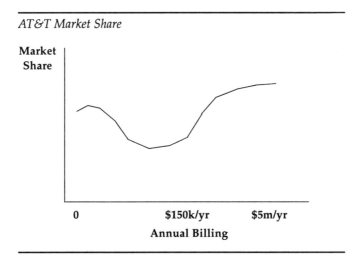

AT&T Market Share

There were two reasons for this gap in the BCS marketing effort. One was that there was no knowledge of what these companies were or where they were located. Though existing AT&T billing records could identify about 15 thousand enterprises in this category, more scientific market analyses indicated that the true number was probably closer to 45 thousand. In many cases, management realized, BCS was losing mid-size customers to other telecommunications suppliers because it wasn't even competing for their business.

Another reason for this strategic oversight was that BCS wasn't set up to sell effectively to the mid-size customer. Traditionally, AT&T's expertise in business sales had always been strongest with large corporations—where account management and relationship development skills are important—and with small companies that are sold to using short-term, transactional selling techniques.

Yet winning over the mid-size customer was critically important to AT&T's market strategy and long-term business objectives. Servicing this fast-growing market segment was essential if AT&T was to maintain a leadership position in the increasingly more competitive telecommunications industry. And since mid-size companies typically spend up to $1 million a year for the kinds of services BCS provides, gaining their business also meant a potentially huge increase in revenues for AT&T.

To make the most of this new business opportunity and, for the first time, to ensure full coverage of the business marketplace, the BCS Middle Markets sales organization was created at the end of 1994. It included twenty-nine branches in four regions and a sales force of over 3,000. One-third of these salespeople were recruited from the existing group that sells to large businesses (Major Markets), one-third were recruited from the BCS group that sells to small businesses (Commercial Markets), and one-third were recruited from outside AT&T.

A New Design and Sales Approach

From the very beginning, Middle Markets was designed in a radically different way from the other sales organizations within BCS. The rationale behind this strategy was clear: If Middle Markets was to succeed, it had to reflect the business needs, buying behaviors, and customer attitudes of these companies and incorporate the kind of sales approach that would work best in selling to them. Several characteristics unique to the mid-size customer had to be taken into consideration.

Business Needs

Mid-size customers do not have the sophisticated voice or data networking requirements of large corporations, but their telecommunications needs are usually more complex than those of small, family-owned companies. Though servicing these accounts rarely requires large selling teams or extensive technical support, the selling cycle for the mid-size customer is usually longer than one sales call and frequently involves more than one decision maker.

Buying Behaviors

In most cases, those who make buying decisions in mid-size companies are not telecommunications specialists. Typically, they rely on simple, clearly written proposals to evaluate vendors, and once the selection has been made, they're strongly dependent on the expertise of the salesperson involved. Consequently, mid-size business customers prefer to deal with salespeople they can trust and relate to, who have extensive knowledge of their organization and industry, and who can offer innovative ideas on how telecommunications can add value to their business and save them money.

Comparative Sales Models

	Small Business Customer	**Mid-Size Business Customer**	**Big Business Customer**
Customer Profile	One decision maker	Multiple decision makers	Complex decision making
Sales Approach	Off-the-shelf product, promotions	Menu-driven, tailored offers	Complex, highly customized
Sales Cycle	One or two calls needed to close	Multiple calls needed to close	Ongoing process to service contract
Sales Support	Low-level technical support	As-needed technical support	High-level technical support
Sales Territory	Geographically defined	Account-assigned modules	Single customer

Customer Attitudes

Like their counterparts in small corporations, buyers in mid-size companies expect timely and effective solutions to their business problems, quick and easy installations, and accurate billing. But like their counterparts in bigger businesses, they also want a personal and ongoing relationship with the salesperson they do business with and expect strong, individualized attention.

Defining Value for Mid-Size Customers

Value =

Knowledge

+

Trust

+

Simplicity

+

Personal Interaction

Selling to the mid-size customer, therefore, required BCS to develop a sales model altogether different from those used in either Major Markets or Commercial Markets. This model would require the BCS salesperson to approach prospects differently and to play a different role once an account was secured—working closely with the customer to uncover business needs, find appropriate solutions for them, and meet needs as they change over time. What's more, this model would have to incorporate elements that could help BCS secure a strong foothold in this new market segment and reach AT&T's ambitious targets for increasing market share.

THE STRUCTURAL COMPONENTS OF CHANGE

To develop the new sales model for Middle Markets, a variety of structural and operating changes were introduced. Among the most basic was the way in which customer account "modules" were created and assigned to salespeople.

Traditionally within BCS, customer accounts and sales resources were allocated on the basis of existing AT&T business. But since one of the primary objectives of Middle Markets was to penetrate a new market, a different approach was taken. Here, each salesperson was assigned a module of between twenty and forty accounts that included AT&T customers as well as companies that were serviced by competitive suppliers. A departure from existing sales structures, this approach was intended to bring about a dramatic shift in the way salespeople viewed their territories by establishing them as account managers whose responsibilities covered not just existing AT&T business but the total business opportunity within their grasp.

Another major structural change was the way in which Human Resource functions—like recruiting, hiring, training, and compensation— were handled. Though these functions had been highly centralized within AT&T in the past, the approach taken in Middle Markets was to administer them locally and to appoint a Human Assets and Learning (HAL) manager at each branch location. Why this change? Since the business needs and organizational characteristics of mid-size companies can vary significantly throughout the United States, it was felt that managers at the branch level should have considerable leeway in deciding what salespeople to hire and how they should be trained to sell to and service the companies in their regions.

The two exceptions to this decentralized approach were S.P.I.N.©, which provided the foundation for selling skills training for all salespeople in Middle Markets, and ACE (Action, Coverage, and Effectiveness). Developed by consultant Neil Rackham, the S.P.I.N. approach to selling is based on the idea that the questioning skills of the salesperson are a critical factor in making successful sales.[1] By asking four specific types of questions, Rackham asserts, salespeople can better uncover hidden or unidentified business needs, develop customized solutions that will improve business performance, and communicate the advantages and benefits of these solutions to the customer. The S.P.I.N. sales technique would be highly effective in Middle Markets, it was believed, because selling opportunities there are strongly based on how well salespeople understand their customer's business situation and can respond effectively to unique customer needs and problems.

S.P.I.N.© Approach to Selling

S*ituation questions*: to understand the customer's industry and business situation.

P*roblem questions*: to create customer awareness of hidden or unidentified needs and problems.

I*mplications questions*: to understand the customer's perception of the impact of problems.

N*eeds payoff questions*: to establish the benefits and advantages of applying a proposed problem solution.

ACE is another interviewing technique that was implemented as a universal training requirement. Unlike S.P.I.N., which is a problem-and-solution-oriented sales approach, the purpose of ACE is to provide the salesperson with a protocol of structured questions that can help evaluate the total business opportunity within an account. Because the amount of business that can be gained from a mid-size customer is not always apparent, ACE was needed to help salespeople set specific targets for each account and develop account penetration strategies, and to make sure that the account modules assigned to salespeople were fairly and evenly apportioned.

New Performance Expectations

Three other components of the BCS reorganization produced significant changes in the way the sales force was managed in Middle Markets and how it was expected to perform. These were "Where's Waldo?," MaxPACE, and financial modeling.

Where's Waldo?

Ever since the breakup of 1984, account identification for the sales organizations within AT&T routinely involved the same process: reviewing company records of existing business customers and of those customers that had been lost. Though this process had served the company well for nearly a decade, one flaw diminished its continued usefulness. It could not identify companies founded after 1984 that had never used AT&T as their telecommunications supplier. Since many of these unknown companies had prospered into mid-size businesses and evolved into the type of customer that Middle Markets was targeting, an effective account identification and prospecting strategy had to be developed. This is the initiative that BCS managers dubbed "Where's Waldo?"

There are two aspects of "Where's Waldo?" that were totally new to AT&T. One is that, remarkably, it was the first prospecting effort ever conducted by the company that did not rely exclusively on AT&T billing records. Instead, a variety of resources outside the company became the primary basis for prospecting and provided the information that was used to uncover potential "Waldos." These included Chamber of Commerce files, building permit applications, state government records, and Dun & Bradstreet data. These resources helped produce an initial list of 900 thousand corporate names, which telemarketers then screened down to 150 thousand companies still in operation.

The second step in the prospecting effort—"qualifying" the companies that had been found as potential Middle Markets customers—was then passed down to the branch level. This was another AT&T first, since sales accounts previously had always been assigned within the company, not selected. Never before had branch managers or sales representatives participated in the process of creating the modules that their compensation was based on. Having them do so this time around, it was believed, would increase feelings of ownership and accountability and establish a greater sense of territorial stewardship.

As it turned out, conducting "Where's Waldo?" as a joint responsibility among the Middle Markets branch offices also had a positive impact on the outcome of the identification process. In the end, some 24 percent more mid-size companies than expected were found, bringing the total amount of untapped business opportunity for AT&T to close to $2 billion.

MaxPACE

Another significant innovation in the Middle Markets sales organization was the way performance was to be managed and rewarded. The objective was to reinforce the notion of a true "performance culture" by focusing on key selling skills and by establishing high performance standards at all levels, especially for the front-line position that occupied the critical "cutting edge" of the organization: the salesperson. Given this orientation, the new performance management approach adopted in Middle Markets was named MaxPACE, an acronym that stood for "Maximum Performance at the Cutting Edge."

Strong management support and extensive coaching were integral parts of the MaxPACE approach. Sales managers would be required to spend 40 percent or more of their time conducting systematic coaching activities: helping to plan account strategies, observing sales calls (at least two each month for every sales rep), and providing regular performance feedback. For those salespeople who continued to underperform, managers were responsible for setting up performance-improvement plans and for monitoring progress on an ongoing basis.

Middle Markets Sales Management: Key Coaching Requirements

Conduct joint planning sessions to estimate business opportunity and set account targets.

Observe each sales rep during at least two calls per month.

Diagnose and evaluate performance in relation to top performers.

Provide feedback on specific sales skills.

Create skill-development plans and review progress quarterly.

Also central to the MaxPACE approach was the concept of "managed churn"—the expectation that a certain percentage of the sales force would probably not make the grade and would have to be let go. Though this was hardly a revolutionary idea, it initially generated considerable anxiety within Middle Markets because it meant that people would be held strictly accountable for their performance and that consistent nonperformers would be weeded out. It also represented a significant departure from the management philosophy that had predominated at AT&T.

Though the performance of salespeople had always been closely monitored within BCS, a sales culture had developed that was characterized by high job security and low turnover. Precise specifications had been established for just about every aspect of the salesperson's job—how much product to sell, how many contacts to approach, when to discuss renewals—and there were detailed reporting requirements. Though this approach helped promote consistency in sales performance, it also created an organizational safety net: Salespeople were considered "competent" as long as they adhered closely to the policies and procedures that were outlined.

The MaxPACE approach removed this safety net for good by giving people more freedom in conducting sales calls but also by holding them more accountable for the results they achieved. Instead of being told exactly what to do and how to do it, from now on salespeople would be evaluated on the basis of a number of new performance criteria: market-share growth, win-back rate, and sales-quota attainment.

Financial Modeling

The third major innovation introduced with Middle Markets was a new way of establishing sales revenue goals called "financial modeling." This would replace the quota system of target setting that was customary within AT&T and that is still a pervasive management practice in sales organizations throughout the country.

One purpose of financial modeling was to eliminate the widespread perception among sales managers that quotas are arbitrarily selected by senior management and that they are subject to negotiation. In many sales organizations, in fact, bargaining sessions are endemic to the target-setting process, where sales managers struggle to convince their bosses that the quotas assigned to them are unrealistic and that they should be revised downward. The result is often an organizational culture in which sales managers and representatives resent their higher-ups and unconsciously undermine efforts to achieve sales targets.

In contrast to this confrontational approach, financial modeling strives to be at once more scientific and more collaborative. Instead of allowing senior management to decide unilaterally what sales targets should be set, financial modeling applies an intricate (though more objective) formula for establishing goals that incorporates branch calculations for a number of variables within each location. Among the many factors taken into consideration were existing AT&T billing, competitive billing, expected account erosion and revenue growth, and potential win-back business.

The intention of this bottom-up approach was to create stronger feelings of financial stewardship and accountability at the local level and to ensure commitment to the new sales organization. Like "Where's Waldo?" and MaxPACE, financial modeling was designed to promote a different mindset among the sales professionals in Middle Markets, and to enhance their effectiveness at winning new customers for AT&T.

PLANNING BEYOND STRUCTURAL CHANGE

This new sales model generated major change in virtually every aspect of the sales function within Middle Markets. Wholesale, top-to-bottom change was, in fact, the primary objective. Just like those organizations that "reengineer" themselves in order to become more efficient and more customer-focused, BCS wanted to completely rethink its old ways of doing business when forming Middle Markets and adopt a more innovative and more productive approach.

Those who work outside the sales arena or in industries unrelated to telecommunications may not comprehend the specific structural

changes that were introduced to create Middle Markets. But business-
people in every field and specialty will understand the imperatives
that propelled those changes. For in most cases, whenever change is
implemented today, the reasons behind it are often the same:

- *To become more competitive*—companies everywhere must now compete in a
  more crowded and more global business marketplace.
- *To create a high-performance organization*—whether in service or in manufacturing, all companies must strive today to improve quality, productivity,
  and customer service.
- *To promote feelings of ownership and accountability*—more companies now realize that long-term success depends on the cooperation and contribution
  of employees at every organizational level.
- *To better meet customer needs*—improving customer satisfaction by responding
  better to increased customer needs and expectations has become the primary
  strategy companies now use to differentiate themselves in the marketplace.
- *To increase market share and bottom-line results*—faced with higher costs and
  stronger competition, companies must work to ensure profitability by becoming more efficient in their business processes, more innovative in their
  marketing efforts, and more effective at managing their people and their
  resources.

It's also important to remember, however, that the changes companies introduce to achieve these objectives inevitably have emotional
consequences. As in the creation of Middle Markets, organizational
change almost always affects people on the most human level and
entails psychological side effects that can be uncomfortable and potentially disruptive. Common emotional responses to change include
increased levels of stress, greater feelings of anxiety, and the strong
temptation to resist or block change.

This is not to say that change should be avoided in business or that
major change is inherently wrong. On the contrary, the need for fundamental change in many companies is indisputable today, and change,
when it's implemented effectively, can produce highly beneficial results. Within BCS, for example, sales revenues for the new Middle
Markets organization after one year exceeded initial targets, and BCS
made significant headway in solidifying its position with the new customers it set out to serve.

But making change succeed requires a clear understanding of its
human impact as well as an effective strategy for dealing with the emotional reactions to it. What managers at BCS learned is that transformation can take place and be sustained only when employees are fully
committed to change emotionally—not just intellectually—and when
both their minds and their hearts are engaged in the change process.

In the following chapters, we'll describe some of the emotional reactions to change at BCS, and how the belief system approach was applied to manage them.

NOTE

1. For more information, see Neil Rackham, *S.P.I.N. Selling* (New York: McGraw-Hill, 1988). Rackham is also the author of *Major Account Sales Strategy* (New York: McGraw-Hill, 1989).

10

Change and Its Emotional Consequences

It was a cold and bleak winter morning in the eastern half of the United States when AT&T's Business Communications Services division launched its Middle Markets sales organization in January 1995. But the bitterness of the weather outside contrasted sharply with the celebratory, almost euphoric mood inside BCS headquarters and its branch offices. The culmination of six months of careful planning, a new organization—fashioned from fourteen discrete change-management initiatives—was being inaugurated, and its creation was commemorated as a hallmark event. Offices were decorated with colored balloons, festive cakes were served with coffee, and a customized music video had been prepared especially for the occasion. To jump-start sales activities, a nationwide teleconference of managers was broadcast to every Middle Markets office. And buoyed by the support and encouragement transmitted from coast to coast, employees began their first day of work with the optimistic feeling that an organizational milestone had been reached.

However, many of the employees who were upbeat and enthusiastic in the morning felt markedly different by late afternoon. After they spent just eight hours at their new jobs, the immense difficulty of the challenges that lay before them suddenly became an uncomfortable reality. They were working for a totally new organization, many now realized—with unknown customers, a new set of job requirements, and higher performance expectations—and there was no turning back.

Over the course of the coming months, the emotional roller coaster ride that many within Middle Markets experienced the day their organization was launched would be repeated numerous times. Just like employees in other organizations that initiate major change, they would undergo the full range of emotions that change produces: from hope and cheerful expectation to fear, anxiety, confusion, and self-doubt.

Some would experience both positive and negative emotions concurrently, a whirling mixture of feelings that were, at the same time, exhilarating and demoralizing. "I felt hopeful because it seemed like we were building a better sales process," one manager later said. "But I was also angry and frustrated because I thought upper management should have involved us more in preparing for change." For others, the good and bad feelings that the change produced were experienced sequentially—a series of emotional peaks and valleys that were spread out over time. This was the case with one newly promoted manager, who recounted, "At first I was excited just to be heading up my own team. But as soon as things got going, I was overwhelmed by feelings of anxiety, because I knew I had to depend on other people to get good results, and pressure, because I wanted to perform as well as my peers. But by the end of the first quarter, I was on top of the world again. My team was doing well, and I felt all charged up. I started to feel that the decisions I was making were really beginning to work."

At BCS, we became aware of these emotions and their patterns through the application of the belief system approach and through interviews conducted with branch managers, sales managers, and sales representatives in the Eastern Region of Middle Markets. But in most companies, change leaders remain unaware of the emotional consequences of their actions, or they underestimate the impact emotions have on change. Even when organizations recognize that change produces powerful emotions—and sometimes even trauma—most of their leaders lack the skills or ability to effectively manage those emotions so that they don't impede or hinder change.

In this chapter, we'll describe the primary emotions that resulted from the launch of Middle Markets and the motivation and performance issues surrounding them. We will show that these emotions are prevalent and pervasive during change, and are common employee reactions that those who implement change must learn to expect, recognize, and manage.

Beliefs and Emotions

As stated in previous chapters, the feelings that employees experience during change can be linked to three types of motivation problems:

1. *Lack of confidence.* When employees are faced with change, they ask themselves the critical question, "Can I do it?" (B-1), and many conclude that they're simply not up to the task. Especially when presented with new job responsibilities, increased production quotas, or unfamiliar practices and procedures, employees often begin to harbor self-doubts and wonder whether the training they received is adequate to do their new job or whether they can deliver the kind of performance that others expect from them.

2. *Lack of trust.* Change can also be the stimulus that leads employees to doubt the connection between what they do at work and what they expect to get from it. Unconsciously they ask, "Will outcomes be tied to my performance?" (B-2), and sometimes conclude that they won't. When promised rewards are not forthcoming, for example, because bonuses or raises have been cut or performance standards aren't clear, then employees begin to question whether the people they work for can really be trusted or whether it's worth putting into their job all the time and effort that's being asked of them.

3. *Lack of satisfaction.* Still another consequence of change is the weakened belief among employees that the things they're working for are things they really want. Assessing the rewards they've been promised, they ask themselves, "Will the outcomes be satisfying to me?" (B-3), and their answer may be "no." When organizations fail to understand the real needs and desires of their people or when too many unwanted outcomes result from change, employees are likely to feel dissatisfied and angry during the change process and lack the motivation to do a good job.

EMOTIONAL PROFILE OF AN ORGANIZATION IN CHANGE

As the belief system approach was implemented throughout the Eastern Region of Middle Markets, it quickly became apparent that all three types of motivation problems were being manifested at every organizational level. Despite the intensive preparation that had gone into selecting high-caliber salespeople and managers, designing a comprehensive sales model and support systems, and locating potentially lucrative customers, no one believed that the success of Middle Markets was assured or that the process of achieving it would be easy.

Insecurity and Self-Doubt

B-1 problems were widespread throughout the organization, because many employees had to develop skills and abilities they never needed before and felt unsure of themselves in their new roles. For example, sales representatives who had previously worked in Major Markets had to become adept at prospecting and qualifying customers and learn how to overcome objections and indifference. Accustomed to working with accounts that were often longtime AT&T customers, this group had to adjust to selling in a marketplace that suddenly seemed far more competitive and unreceptive.

Sales representatives from Commercial Markets also had new and difficult skills to master, such as writing detailed and compelling sales proposals and managing a much longer sales cycle. Skilled at conducting quick-hit sales that were often completed in a single day, this group had to develop the patience and perseverance required in selling to larger companies, the teamwork skills involved in servicing more complex accounts, and the special capabilities needed to maintain long-term customer relationships.

Caring for the Mid-Size Customer

What to do	Build and maintain the customer relationship.
	Help the customer get the job done.
	Improve the customer's business performance.
How to do it	Through a designated team approach: Sales Representative, Technical Support, Customer Service Technician, and Sales Manager.

Sales managers from every background had problems applying the new financial model introduced at the branch level (see Chapter 9), and this caused considerable anxiety and confusion in the months immediately following the launch. Even those who retained the advanced math skills they learned in college lacked confidence in applying the model, and almost all were loath to admit their shortcomings and self-doubts.

Image and Identity Issues

Though not as prevalent, B-2 problems also surfaced at every level with the creation of Middle Markets. Unlike in many other organizations that change, where these problems typically result from the introduction of new compensation systems that are perceived as unfair or from cutbacks in raises, trust-related issues at BCS (and feelings that "I'm not getting what I deserve") had more to do with image and prestige than with money.

Both Major Markets and Commercial Markets were established sales organizations within BCS, and each had its own history of achievement and recognized corporate identity: Those who worked in Major Markets felt pride in associating with big-name AT&T accounts, while those in Commercial Markets were admired for their ability to execute quick transaction sales. But Middle Markets had as yet no defined self-image, so at first many of its employees—especially those coming from other parts of AT&T—perceived their new position as a reduction in organizational status.

The initial obstacles that salespeople and their managers had to overcome to win mid-size customers did little to dispel the belief that Middle Markets was the least desirable sales organization to belong to. Instead of leading to enhanced feelings of accomplishment and self-respect, these challenges at first caused many to look upon their move to Middle Markets almost as a punishment (a "booby prize"), rather than a reward, for all their previous years of hard work. Particularly among high achievers, the feeling that they had been deceived or tricked into joining Middle Markets was common. Though most didn't say so openly, many sales representative and managers started to think, "I've done a great job for this company, and now I'm being 'rewarded' by being stuck in Middle Markets."

Accompanying these feelings of second-class corporate citizenship were B-3 issues at every organizational level, indicating that many Middle Markets employees didn't enjoy or like their new jobs. As is often the case when organizations change, the discomfort that people feel in trying to do something new is often interpreted as an antipathy to the job itself. And since many sales managers and account representatives had been drafted into Middle Markets—and not given a choice about their new assignment—there were growing feelings after the launch that "This isn't what I like to do" or "I'm not really cut out for this."

Symptoms of Motivation Problems

B-1   "I can't do it."
        "I don't think we can pull this off."
        "I don't have enough training for this."

B-2   "I deserve better than this."
        "Is this what I get for all my years of hard work?"
        "I don't think this is fair."

B-3   "This isn't what I thought my job would be."
        "I'm just not cut out for this kind of work."
        "I'm not sure how long I can do this."

Panic and Confusion

Not surprisingly, these emotions and feelings were strongest during the first few months after the launch of Middle Markets, when employees were still adjusting to their new jobs and many hadn't developed the proficiency they needed to perform their work with confidence and skill. "So much was going on at that time that nothing got the attention it deserved," one manager recalled of this period. "Most of us were still trying to figure things out—the new compensation plan, personnel stuff, and the training requirements—and nobody was telling us what to do. It was unsettling at first, and scary."

As in any major change effort, these emotions can be exacerbated when the change goes on longer than expected (a common occurrence in organizational transformations), or when obstacles arise that could not have been predicted before the change effort was initiated. This is precisely what happened in Middle Markets when, in preparing for the startup, management made a mistake in calculating the expected length of the sales cycle and underestimated it by about half.

Originally, the sales cycle for mid-size customers was expected to last about six weeks. But once operations got under way, it was soon apparent that salespeople actually needed at least twice that long to close a typical sale. Since so many variables are affected by the length of the sales cycle—most importantly, commissions and revenues—this created confusion and even panic among salespeople in the early months after the launch. Some took their inability to close sales quickly as a sign of their incompetence (B-1), while others feared it meant diminished personal incomes (B-2). For those who entered Middle Markets reluctantly, it confirmed their belief that they had made the wrong job choice (B-3).

As it turned out, Middle Markets would by year's end become the best-paying sales organization within BCS. But there was no way of knowing that in the early months of 1995, and the concerns caused by a longer-than-expected sales cycle threatened to undermine the change effort and eat away at whatever enthusiasm and excitement had been generated by the launch. "One of my people left early when he realized he wasn't going to make money right away," one manager remembers. "If he had stayed, he would have done all right. But there was a tremendous emotional reaction when people thought they weren't going to make the money they hoped for. For some, it was panic. For others frustration, and a sinking feeling that their job would be even harder than they expected."

SPECIAL MOTIVATION PROBLEMS

Though issues related to confidence, trust, and satisfaction were apparent at all levels after the startup of Middle Markets, each level also experienced emotions and motivation problems that were unique to its role in the organization and that had to be managed effectively if the transformation was to take hold and succeed.

Sales Representatives

B-1 problems were especially common among sales representatives, because the new sales model they had to apply was in many cases a radical departure from the selling process they were used to. For this group, there were increased feelings of uncertainty and self-doubt, and sometimes even fear.

Representatives who formerly worked in Commercial Markets had become accustomed to selling relatively simple products. To be effective in Middle Markets, they had to come up with sometimes complicated and highly technical solutions to customer problems, and demonstrate an intimate familiarity with the broad spectrum of AT&T products. Sales representatives from Major Markets, used to working as part of a large and dedicated team, now found themselves with considerably less support and with no guaranteed customers or commissions.

Sales Managers

B-1 problems were also prevalent among sales managers, who now had to develop new skills in territory planning and module construction, and B-3 issues were common as well, particularly as a result of the MaxPACE approach. The predominant feelings in this group were stress and insecurity.

Many sales managers felt uncomfortable managing in a true "performance culture." In the past, effort and hard work had been rewarded in BCS; now the emphasis was on results, and those who couldn't deliver had to be coached, or else managed out of the organization, leading some sales managers to think, "I'm not really sure I can do this."

Key Sales Rep Skills

Opportunity identification & planning

Questioning & selling

Product value delivery

Systems applications

Key Sales Manager Skills

Coaching

Executive selling

Managing office & staff

Also, the idea of monitoring their people closely and of letting people go wasn't consistent with what some managers felt their job would be when they first joined BCS. Working in a far more demanding sales environment, some reacted negatively and emotionally. "My behavior style makes it difficult for me to function in a performance culture," one manager acknowledged. "MaxPACE didn't make sense to me, and when change requires things that don't make sense, your emotions surface."

Branch Managers

The shift in responsibilities among branch managers also gave rise to B-1 and B-3 problems. They were now asked to participate more in quota setting, meet more difficult profit and growth targets, and know vastly more about their customers and competitors. Understandably, this generated feelings of anxiety, confusion, and even inadequacy, as many began to question their abilities and self-worth.

Some branch managers weren't used to operating at the level of autonomy that was now expected of them as part of the Middle Markets sales organization. Without the clearly defined policies and procedures that were part of the old BCS culture, some felt they weren't getting enough support from their organization or that their job requirements were excessive or unrealistic. Among those who had to develop stronger financial management skills—both to apply the complicated financial model that was now used to set sales and growth targets and to meet the organization's ambitious profit goals—some began to question their intellectual capacities and ability to change.

TWO GROUPS THAT CHANGE HITS HARDEST

Special motivation problems also arose in Middle Markets among the two groups of employees who typically bear the greatest emotional burden during change: newly promoted employees and first-level managers.

Though it's common for organizations to attempt to infuse new talent into their management ranks at the time they undergo change, this puts a dual burden on those who are promoted as part of the change effort. Like everyone else, they must adjust to a new work environment, with new values, new procedures, and new organizational objectives. But they must also learn an entirely new job in the process and deal with increased demands and expectations. Compounding this problem is the fact that many newly promoted employees are high achievers who are reluctant to acknowledge their problems or weaknesses. In many change situations, they will forge ahead against considerable odds and refuse to ask for help, even when they feel inside that they may be sinking.

This was the case with one sales manager in Middle Markets who had previously been a highly successful sales representative in BCS. Though he later admitted that he was having serious problems with the change and with carrying out the responsibilities of his new position, he hid his true feelings for months—until his one-on-one session. In a stunning revelation to his branch manager, this former sales representative broke down and cried several times during their meeting, when he finally disclosed how he really felt about his job.

Emotional reactions this strong are also not uncommon among first-level managers, as our experience with Middle Markets showed. The primary reason is that even when those who hold these positions are not new to management, they must often adjust to jobs that have been radically altered or redesigned. In many cases, their span of control has been dramatically increased, the way they spend their time is significantly different, and the performance standards and measures they must apply undergo major modifications.

Two other factors complicate the way in which first-level managers respond emotionally to change. One is that, unlike their superiors, these supervisors are less likely to have been involved in designing and preparing for the new organization they must work in. Consequently, they have less time to adjust mentally to the changes that are implemented and are less motivated to embrace them. The other, and perhaps more significant, factor is that first-level managers always absorb some emotional "spillover" from the people they manage. As firsthand witnesses to the psychological turmoil that change creates, they cannot ignore the human impact of change and are often affected emotionally by what it does to those around them.

One Middle Markets sales manager, for example, said he developed nearly debilitating anxieties when his team realized their sales cycle would be longer than they expected. "The worst part of my job was keeping my people from crashing for fear of not being able to close their sales fast enough," he said. "I constantly had to tell myself not to panic when they were having performance problems. Though money was really not an issue for me, I became more and more anxious just from watching what my people were going through."

Since first-level managers play pivotal roles as organizational go-betweens and interpreters of change, helping them to cope with change and its emotional manifestations should be a top priority for every organization that undertakes a major change effort.

CLASSIC CHANGE MANAGEMENT VERSUS THE NEW CHANGE MODEL

The emotional reactions that we have described as part of the Middle Markets start-up are common—even normal—responses to the disruptive power of change and its ability to alter people's lives. Though the degree of emotional impact may vary among organizations (depending on the extent of change involved, the adaptability of each organization, and the desire for change), change always has emotional consequences that, if left unmanaged, can be detrimental.

Naturally, not all the emotions associated with change are negative or destructive. For some employees, organizational change can be positive and uplifting: It may bring welcome relief from a job they never liked, for example, or sever for good their connection to a boss they never got along with. Change can also offer new professional opportunities, add excitement to workday routines, and present challenges that, when met, can lead to increased feelings of pride and self-confidence. As one BCS manager told us, "For me, moving to Middle Markets was a real opportunity—it was where I wanted to be. Sure, it meant hard work and stress. But it was a good kind of stress, and I was never so excited in my life."

It should be remembered, however, that even when change is implemented relatively smoothly the kind of emotions that it usually produces are, at best, mixed. Rarely do employees anticipate proposed changes at work with unadulterated enthusiasm, nor are they likely to see change as simply a chance to expand their professional horizons or prove their mettle to higher-ups. Though there were employees who said they felt excited and hopeful about the change in the interviews we conducted after the launch of Middle Markets, negative descriptors—like "difficult," "overwhelming," "painful," and "intense"—were far more common. One manager even admitted, "For the twelve months of 1995, I was terrified at work every single day."

Increased Memos and Meetings

In Middle Markets, the initial management strategy for helping employees to cope with change was to apply traditional and widely practiced change-management techniques, such as increased communication and one-on-one coaching. Relying on the advice of those experts who proclaim the curative power of communication and coaching ("It's impossible to overcommunicate during change," some experts argue), management's first attempt at moderating the impact of change in the final quarter of 1994 was to issue more memos, conduct more meetings, and make sure each employee had access to a coach.

With hindsight, however, it isn't difficult to see why such measures had little overall impact. Though communication is always essential in business organizations—and especially during change—the types of communications that corporations typically resort to when in transition tend to be top down, information based, and broadcast oriented. No matter how clear or well organized they are, memos and meetings that are designed to communicate change often fail to get through to employees because they don't address the emotions of change. What's more, many employees don't hear what is being communicated because they're preoccupied with precisely those fears and anxieties that these communications are intended to overcome.

While often necessary, one-on-one coaching is also an insufficient strategy for managing the wide-ranging emotional consequences of change, as the Middle Markets experience showed. Designed to address specific skill or product-knowledge deficiencies, coaching may eliminate some motivation and performance problems (B-1 issues, for example), but it is an inadequate mechanism for dealing with the many other emotional issues that may arise during change: loss of job security, diminished job status, or the feelings associated with changes in job content.

With the belief system approach, however, Middle Markets gained an effective tool for communicating to employees the organizational imperative for change, and showing how that imperative fits within the context of each employee's emotional and psychological framework. Over time, this resulted in a greater understanding and acceptance of change, and enhanced the organization's ability to implement change successfully.

In Chapter 11 we will describe in detail how the belief system was implemented at the highest management levels within the Eastern Region of Middle Markets, and demonstrate the effectiveness of this approach in facilitating change.

11

Initiating the Change Process

Of all the managers who work in mainstream business functions, those in charge of sales are the most familiar with motivation improvement. Since motivation has always been considered a key to success in selling, improving motivation has become an integral component of the sales manager's job and a major focus of management attention. This does not mean that sales managers are eager to try every new motivation improvement technique that comes along. On the contrary, because they've been subjected to so many improvement programs throughout their careers, many sales managers are skeptical of new motivation techniques and are reluctant to invest the time and energy that many of them require.

This is one reason why, when the decision was made to introduce the belief system to the Eastern Region of Middle Markets, no directives regarding the approach were issued and no branch managers were required to implement it. Instead, the belief system was introduced as a possible solution to the change-related problems occurring in the organization, which every branch manager was aware of and recognized.

Branch Management Profile

Covering thirteen states and the District of Columbia, the Eastern Region consists of eight branch offices that, together, account for about one-third of all Middle Markets revenues and customers. Headed by a branch manager, each office targets up to 2,500 business customers, services accounts worth close to $200 million, and employs anywhere from 80 to 120 people. About half the employees at the branch level are sales representatives; the other half are administrative support personnel, technical experts, and management staff. Besides the branch manager, this group includes a human assets & learning manager (HAL), a branch systems manager (BSM), a business operations manager (BOM), and a field marketing manager (FMM).

Eastern Region Branch Managers

Number:	8
Sex:	5 males, 3 females
Race:	7 whites, 1 black
AT&T experience:	0–30 years
Branch manager experience:	0–11 years

Though the Eastern Region covers some of the wealthiest and most industrialized states in America, it was not considered the most promising sales region within Middle Markets at the time the organization was launched. With a political climate unfriendly to big business and a declining manufacturing base, the Eastern Region was the last to emerge from the 1990–1991 recession, had the slowest-growing economy of the four Middle Markets regions, and faced off against some of AT&T's biggest and strongest rivals. Indeed, MCI, Frontier Communications, ATX, and LCI all have their headquarters in this territory.

What the Eastern Region did have in its favor, however, was a strong leadership team of branch managers who possessed extensive experience and superior talent. Five had previously worked as branch managers within BCS, most had a long history with AT&T, and all were high achievers. Though their personality styles varied considerably—from boisterous and outgoing to cerebral and quiet—each was strongly committed to the change effort and to making Middle Markets a BCS success. Their boss, Sales Vice President Ray Butkus (coauthor of this book), served previously as a Sales Vice President in Major Markets and had worked in the telecommunications industry for twenty-one years, eighteen of them with AT&T.

INTRODUCING THE NEW APPROACH

The belief system was first introduced to branch managers at a routine staff meeting for the Eastern Region held in late 1994. Though it was positioned as a possible solution to the emotional problems caused by the change and as a technique to uncover their root causes, the decision to use the new approach was left entirely to each branch manager. Not surprisingly, this proposal elicited a wide range of reactions, from welcome enthusiasm to cautious acceptance and skepticism.

As in any group of managers, there were those few "early adapters" who were favorably disposed to the change-management tool, convinced of its merit, and eager to use it. Their overall response was, "It sounds great to us. What have we got to lose? Let's give it a try." At the other end of the spectrum were those branch managers who harbored serious doubts about the approach, but agreed to go along with it if it pleased their boss. "You're in charge," was the attitude they projected. "If you want us to use this, we will. But don't blame us if it doesn't work." Most of the branch managers adopted a wait-and-see attitude. Though they weren't totally convinced of the value of the approach, they were willing to put aside their doubts temporarily and to give it a try. "Maybe there's something here, maybe there isn't," was their communal response. "But whatever the case, we're willing to go along with it for now and see what happens."

Though almost all the branch managers would eventually become ardent advocates of the belief system (and seven of the eight would implement it), their initial impressions were slow to change. At the end of the two-day learning session, in fact, most appeared no more enthusiastic about the approach than they were at the staff meeting. "I have to say that my reaction to the training session was not a very positive one," a manager later admitted. "I was so concerned about how this tool would be implemented that I really couldn't focus on its value."

This response is not uncommon whenever the belief system is introduced to organizations. For despite the importance of the training session in outlining the four-part process and providing the theory to explain why it works, the power of the approach usually does not become apparent until managers and their subordinates actually go through it. "I liked the idea of the belief system when it was explained to us during the two-day session. But I wasn't totally convinced that it would work," one manager later said. "I understood it intellectually, but not emotionally."

One typical result of the training session is increased apprehension about what the process entails—in particular, the one-on-one session where managers and their direct reports meet and, guided by a facili-

---

The Four-Part Process

Two-day training session. The manager and his or her direct reports meet to learn the belief system methodology and how to use it.

One-on-one (application) session. Following the two-day training session, the manager meets individually with each direct report, in the presence of a trained facilitator, to identify and solve motivation and performance problems.

Team meeting. When all the one-on-one sessions have been completed, the facilitator conducts a group meeting with the manager and his or her direct reports to discuss the overall results of the sessions and plan changes.

Follow-up sessions. The approach is kept alive by the manager and his or her direct reports in follow-up sessions (usually every six months) that review written commitments.

---

tator, discuss specific motivation and performance problems. For the branch managers this seemed to represent a double jeopardy: Each would have to go through a one-on-one session with their manager (the Sales Vice President) and then with each of the managers they supervised.

When people realize that the one-on-one session is a requirement—not an option—it often gives rise to feelings of anxiety. Frequently, they will ask themselves, "Will it really be safe for me to talk honestly with my boss? Am I willing to take this risk and reveal how I truly feel? How much should I say, and how will my boss react to it? Do I have the courage to hear what my subordinates will tell me?" Usually coupled with this anxiety, however, is the more reassuring feeling and hopeful expectation that the one-on-one session will be a positive and liberating experience, that it will provide an opportunity to verbalize feelings and concerns, and that it will get to the root of troubling motivation and performance problems.

IMPLEMENTING THE ONE-ON-ONE SESSIONS

The first one-on-one sessions were held in the Eastern Region in January 1995. With Thad Green as facilitator, these sessions were conducted between the Sales Vice President and each of his branch managers and executive staff members. As expected, the content and results of these sessions varied widely, though in almost every case significant emotions surfaced and several issues related to motivation and performance were raised, discussed, and resolved.[1]

Some of these issues were B-1 problems stemming from the introduction of new organizational systems, particularly the complicated financial model, the modified compensation plan, and the performance management approach called MaxPACE (see Chapter 9). Though B-1 problems were far more common among sales managers and sales representatives, there were those among the competent and seasoned business professionals who comprised the branch manager group who said they found it difficult to cope with the number and extent of the changes being made and were beginning to lose their self-confidence.

Motivation and Performance Problems

B-1: Can I do it?
B-2: Will outcomes be tied to my performance?
B-3: Will outcomes be satisfying to me?

One high-level staff member demonstrated these feelings of insecurity, for example, when she revealed during her session that her primary reason for coming to work each day "is to prove to myself that I'm not stupid." This startling comment, coming from a highly educated woman who was widely respected for her abilities and intelligence, shows how quickly self-doubts can emerge—even among the highest ranked and most talented—in an environment where change is rapid and expectations are high.

Two other branch managers also indicated during their sessions that they were having significant B-1 problems when they asked the Sales Vice President to "slow down" in introducing new concepts and systems. Not everyone learns at the same speed, they each reminded him, an important message for organizational leaders to remember when implementing change.

The sessions with these two managers raised another important point: The same systems leaders introduce to bring about improvement can cause trauma and increase feelings of self-doubt even at the highest levels, and this can undermine a change effort by reducing management effectiveness overall. At a time when managers need to be performing at their best, the fears and uncertainties they feel during change often make them perform at their worst.

Career-Altering Sessions

By far, most of the issues raised by branch managers during their one-on-one sessions were B-3 problems. One major reason was that the significant changes in their jobs brought about by the creation of Middle Markets led a number of branch managers to reevaluate their careers and the level of satisfaction they received from their work.

In one case, the B-3 issues involved were significant enough to lead to a total career change. This branch manager said he came to feel frustrated and dissatisfied with his job during the transformation and, in a highly emotional one-on-one session that lasted more than four hours, admitted that he felt he could make a bigger contribution to BCS in another capacity. Motivated and exceptionally competent, this manager said he began the belief system process thinking he could be happy with his job if a few minor changes were made to it. But the process involved so much soul searching, he explained, that it made him realize that what he really wanted to do was something entirely different. Eventually, he was reassigned to a part of AT&T that was not going through such accelerated change and where he was able to participate in management activities that interested him more: business strategy, policy formulation, and capital investments.

In another case, the one-on-one session helped a branch manager to achieve peace of mind by allowing him to verbalize his wish *not* to be offered a more prestigious job. This manager had been living happily with his wife and children in a small suburban community, and for many years had willingly undertaken an arduous commute simply not to have to relocate his family. Now that he was a branch manager, he said, he felt increased pressure to work toward a position at headquarters and actually feared that he would be offered a promotion.

Given the chance to express these feelings during his one-on-one session, however, this manager was able to explain to his boss exactly what kind of recognition he wanted for doing his job well: Periodic public pats on the back and the opportunity to contribute to his team were fine, he said, but he'd gladly pass on any opportunity to move up the organizational ladder and onto headquarters.

Relationship-Altering Sessions

In the vast majority of cases, the B-3 problems raised by branch managers during their one-on-one sessions were important, but not career altering. Often, they represented persistent and nagging problems whose resolution made a considerable difference to the branch managers' motivation and performance and to their working relationship with the Sales Vice President.

In one session, for example, the major issue raised by the branch manager had to do with her boss's tendency to solve her problems for her. Though some managers might welcome this kind of intervention, this branch manager felt quite differently. She found it an irritating habit, she said, and one that reflected badly on her ability to manage. "When I come to you with a problem, it's not because I want you to solve it for me," she told him in exasperation. "It's simply because I want to think out loud with you. And I want to be able to do that without the fear that you're making the judgment that, because I've voiced a problem, I need you to solve it for me and I'm incapable of solving it—neither of which is true."

At first the Sales Vice President was reluctant to admit that he responded to her in this way. But after the branch manager provided a number of specific examples to demonstrate this behavior, he had to admit that she was right. To resolve the issue, both agreed that the branch manager would use the code phrase, "Ray, I want to think out loud with you," whenever she wanted to discuss a problem. And after that session, she used the phrase dozens of times in interactions with her boss.

This simple change in the system of communication between these two people had a significant and positive impact on their overall working relationship. But it also reaffirms an important aspect of the belief system approach: Resolving problems is a *joint* process—the boss cannot do it alone—and it often requires employee commitment and follow-through.

In another one-on-one session, a branch manager complained that too little had been done to accommodate her unique and sometimes eccentric management style. A consummate sales professional with a proven track record, this manager said she felt constrained by the guidelines issued during the change and was opposed to any doctrinaire approach to managing her people. "Just tell me the results you want, and let me deliver them my way," she told her boss. "If you're really interested in motivating me, you'll not only acknowledge that I do things differently, but give me credit for it."

A similar example had to do with two branch managers whose personality styles were significantly different from those of their peers and who felt disadvantaged because of it. Reticent and reserved by nature, these managers each asked during their one-on-one session that the Sales Vice President actively solicit their comments during staff meetings and not presume that they would automatically speak up. "You shouldn't just conclude that I have an opinion, and expect me to jump in," they each said in their own way. "I'm not that kind of person. If you want to know what I think, you have to ask me."

The Sales Vice President was more than willing to agree to this request, but on one condition: Each of these branch managers must also agree to undertake some behavioral change. "From now on, I resolve to actively seek out your input," he promised each manager. "But you've got to understand that I won't remember to do that all the time, and that you will sometimes have to remind me." Following those sessions, these two managers participated more fully in staff meetings and contributed to improving the overall decision-making process for the branch manager team.

Reasonable Requests, Simple Solutions

What do these problems have to do with the changes in BCS? Though issues linked to the change effort were brought up repeatedly during the one-on-one sessions, there were instances when no direct causation could be established between the problems raised by the branch managers and the launch of Middle Markets. Still, this does not mean that the problems and the change effort were unrelated. How so? Because underlying or ongoing work problems are more likely to surface during times of change, when tensions run high and everyday problems seem especially troublesome to the people who experience them.

Most employees are more than willing to talk about these problems if they feel safe in doing so. But even when mechanisms exist to promote better communication at work—like performance reviews or suggestion systems—employees seldom view them as opportunities to express their feelings or to talk about work issues that affect them personally. With the belief system approach, however, these sensitive work issues can be addressed tactfully and effectively, and in an atmosphere of collaborative problem solving.

For managers, giving employees the opportunity to reveal how they truly feel can be a daunting prospect. Many of them expect the worst from their one-on-one sessions and fear that they will have to confront unrealistic demands that they won't be able to meet. But in reality this rarely happens. In the vast majority of cases, as the examples show, the issues employees raise are relatively minor from the manager's perspective (though certainly not from the employee's) and readily solvable. Though managers often expect employees to ask for a major promotion or a substantial increase in salary, the things that employees say they need in order to perform better or to become more motivated are usually quite modest: additional recognition, more satisfying assignments, and increased feedback.

What's more, using the belief system approach, employees are encouraged to come up with their own solutions to problems, and most of these solutions are practical, easy to implement, and inexpensive. Rather than complicating managers' lives, as many at first expect, the approach actually relieves managers of the responsibility for solving every work-related problem and helps them improve motivation and performance in a relatively quick and easy way.

ESTABLISHING PERFORMANCE EXPECTATIONS

While the one-on-one sessions helped to resolve many of the personal work issues that had been on the minds of the eight branch managers, they also served another important purpose: to help establish performance expectations during the change, for both the branch managers and the Sales Vice President. "Some people found during their one-on-ones that the roles they were supposed to play were different than they originally thought," one manager later said. "When jobs are new, or the people assigned to them are new, the belief system approach can really help."

In one case, for example, the one-on-one session uncovered a major disconnect between a branch manager's perception of his job and that of the Sales Vice President. This manager was meeting his quotas in only three of four critical job categories. Though he felt he was performing adequately and didn't have to worry about performance improvement, the Sales Vice President found this situation unacceptable. To him, it meant that the branch manager was carrying out only 75 percent of his job, at best, and that there was considerable room for improvement.

Here, the one-on-one session helped reveal a significant performance problem: Either the branch manager did not have the skills or ability to carry out the job that was expected of him (a B-1 problem), or he lacked a clear understanding of his complete job and the repercussions of not performing it (a B-2 problem). Though a solution to either problem might have been found, what complicated the issue was the branch manager's refusal to admit that a problem even existed. Unilaterally, he had come to the conclusion that his performance was satisfactory, despite the poor rating that his boss had given him.

In the face of this resistance, the Sales Vice President felt he had no choice but to "level bold" with this branch manager (see Chapter 2). In essence, he told him, "You have a performance problem, neither one of us has come up with a workable solution, and I am not willing to live with this problem any longer." Failing to respond to this shape-up-or-ship-out message, the branch manager eventually lost his position and was reassigned elsewhere within the company.

Breaking Behavioral Patterns

One-on-one sessions help to clarify expectations for both parties, and managers sometimes learn that they must operate differently in order to implement change better or to increase their subordinates' desire to perform. This was true in the sessions conducted with branch managers for the Eastern Region, which helped raise the consciousness of the Sales Vice President by highlighting certain behaviors that his direct reports felt were counterproductive.

In almost every session, for example, branch managers mentioned their boss's tendencies to use abrupt, direct language and to judge too quickly. This behavior was intimidating and unsettling, the branch managers told him. It increased their stress levels, reduced their effectiveness, and caused them to be less candid in their interactions with him. Though the Sales Vice President was unaware of many of these patterns and of their negative impact, he agreed during the team meeting following the sessions that he would attempt to modify his management style and strive for greater sensitivity.

Illuminating behavioral patterns like these, particularly those demonstrated by managers, is a common outcome of the belief system approach. Though some managers might interpret this feedback as "manager bashing," most welcome the information they receive from subordinates as constructive criticism that they can use to develop themselves professionally. In many cases, it allows them to look at themselves in a new light and to identify behaviors that they can change in order to become more effective managers.

Managing to the Individual

This kind of feedback is especially valuable during a change effort, when managers often need to make adjustments in their supervisory styles. There are times, for example, when those who normally practice a hands-off approach find that they need to be more directive and more involved. At other times, managers who are typically authoritative and hard driving—an approach that may work effectively during "normal" times—find that their people need a different approach during change and that a collaborative or nurturing style is more productive. One Middle Markets manager, for example, later said that he felt the change effort in BCS would have gone more smoothly if senior management had been less "paternalistic" and more "participative." "Increased involvement would have made a big difference," he said.

One of the most important lessons managers learn from their one-on-one sessions, however, is that no single management style works effectively every time and for all subordinates. Management is, by definition, a people-intensive process, and people are, by definition, individuals. Yet many managers tend to apply a "cookie-cutter" approach to supervision and to treat all subordinates as if they were the same. Through the belief system process, they learn how each subordinate needs to be managed, which management approaches produce the best results, and when they should be applied.

Employees, too, usually develop a more informed understanding of their managers during one-on-one sessions, and this helps them to make adjustments in how they interact with others at work. "If I had gone through this process when I first started my job, I would have known better what was expected of me, and things would not have seemed so hard," one manager explained. "My boss and I would probably have had a better relationship, and that would have reduced a lot of the anger and frustration I felt at the time."

EARLY CHANGE RESULTS

Implementing the belief system process in the early months after the launch of Middle Markets helped BCS to create a more effective senior management team, and it improved working relationships at the highest level. The Sales Vice President came away from the one-on-one sessions with a deeper knowledge of the strengths and weaknesses of his branch managers and how he had to adjust his management style with each one. The branch managers came away with a stronger awareness of what their boss expected of them, and with the reassuring feeling that their problems had been listened to and addressed. "We became much more of a real team," one branch manager later said, "and that even includes the renegades." The belief system process was able to promote this by

- identifying the change-related issues that troubled each branch manager and resolving each issue individually.
- finding solutions to motivation and performance problems before they could escalate and become major impediments to change.
- improving communication among members of the senior management team at a time when frequent and open interactions are crucial to organizational success.

The one-on-one sessions with the branch managers initiated a process of improvement that would continue during the change effort and cascade throughout the organization. Even before one-on-one sessions were implemented among sales managers and sales representatives, the positive results from the work with branch managers would produce ripple-like effects that would impact virtually everyone in the Eastern Region. For when behavioral change occurs at the top, it changes more than just the leadership team: "When my branch manager's relationship with her boss changed, she began to treat us differently. And that changed the way I deal with my own people," one sales manager later said.

In the following chapter, we'll look at how the belief system was implemented throughout the Eastern Region of Middle Markets and describe its impact on sales managers and sales representatives.

NOTE

1. It should be noted that predesigned instruments were used in the implementation of the belief system in the Eastern Region, including the Belief System Profile, the Self-Diagnosis of Motivation/Performance Problem, the Preferred Motivation Environment, and the Behavioral Style Analysis. This is one reason why the one-on-one sessions with branch managers were able to focus on specific motivation and performance problems, which were identified before the sessions began. For a description of these instruments and how they can be used, see Chapter 7.

12

Cascading Change

If there's one principle that guides the entire belief system approach, it's the idea that managing is a shared responsibility, not just the boss's job. Employees cannot solve their motivation and performance problems without the cooperation of their managers, and managers cannot solve their employees' problems without the cooperation of the people who have them.

Employees are the best source of solutions to their own problems, so they must be brought into the management equation to achieve optimal results. This is the reason why managers and their direct reports are trained together in the belief system approach. In contrast to traditional training practices which exclude bosses whenever their subordinates are trained, we take the position that there's no team when one party or the other is absent from the playing field.

Following the training, the belief system then gently directs managers and their subordinates to communicate openly with each other and to apply what they've learned in the one-on-one session. With a trained facilitator present to guide the discussion, this is when managers and their direct reports meet face to face, up close and live, in a systematic effort to identify motivation and performance problems, determine their root causes, and come up with effective solutions.

Learning through Repetition

Repetition and continuity are the ways the belief system ensures that the notion of shared responsibility becomes a routine management practice. In most organizations, participants pass through the process twice, first as a direct report (with their manager) and then as a manager (with each one of the people they supervise).

Cascading the Belief System

X		4th Level Manager
	X	3rd Level Manager
2nd Level Manager	X	
1st Level Manager		X
Hourly employees		X

The mechanism that provides this repetition is what we call cascading (see Chapter 7). This is a critical step in the implementation of the belief system approach, and one that ensures that the benefits of the process are realized throughout the organization. Though cascading often takes weeks to complete, and sometimes even months, it is only through cascading that the belief system has the power to change things for the better in the workplace and ensure that individual improvement translates into organizational success.

In the case of Middle Markets, the belief system cascade started with the Sales Vice President of the Eastern Region and with his team of branch managers (see Chapter 11).

THE LOGISTICS OF CASCADING

Cascading the belief system change model throughout the Eastern Region began in the spring of 1995, shortly after the process was implemented at the senior management level. In most branch offices, cascading was carried out in two phases. Branch managers conducted one-on-one application sessions with their sales managers; then sales managers conducted one-on-one sessions with the sales representatives they supervised.

This meant that a typical branch manager who implemented the process completed a total of ten to thirteen one-on-one sessions: one session with the Sales Vice President, one with each of the six to eight sales managers in the branch, and one with each of the four staff managers in the branch. A typical sales manager completed eight to ten sessions: one session with the branch manager, and one session with each of the sales representatives on his or her team.

Cascading took from three to six months within each branch, depending on the time of year, the schedules of the participants, and their eagerness to implement the process. As at the senior-management level, the decision to implement the belief system within sales teams was left entirely to each sales manager. In some branches, the approach was implemented within almost every sales team; in others, it was implemented by only a few teams or by none at all.

Two factors seemed to play a major role in the decision to implement the belief system. One was the experience of the branch managers in the sessions conducted with their subordinates. For example, if a branch manager had been through especially difficult or emotionally draining one-on-one sessions, this would sometimes have an adverse impact on the sales managers in the branch and lead them to decide against implementation. They would ask themselves, "Do I really want to go through this process myself?" or "Am I ready to face the kind of criticism that I gave my own boss?"

Organizational performance was another factor. If a branch or sales team was doing well, it was sometimes decided that the belief system wasn't really necessary. In one Eastern Region branch where sales revenues exceeded 200 percent of quota, for example, many of the sales managers decided to forgo the process.

Not every organization needs to implement the belief system. Though just about everyone can benefit from the approach, it requires an investment in time and energy that for some may simply not be cost-effective. While even top-notch organizations will see some improvement with the process, the belief system works best in organizations that are in pain: those that are experiencing pervasive motivation and performance problems, those that are unable to deliver expected results, or those that are going through a period of emotional upheaval as a result of change.

A FOCUS ON MANAGEMENT STYLE

As we stated in the last chapter, the belief system may also be beneficial when the management style of an organizational leader is inconsistent with what subordinates want or with what is needed during a change effort. This was the case in several branches of the Eastern Region of Middle Markets, and it was the focus of discussion in a number of the one-on-one sessions conducted between branch managers and their direct reports.

In one case, a branch manager heard from his subordinates that his aggressive and overbearing style made them feel anxious at work and interfered with their effectiveness as sales managers. In a series of long and highly emotional one-on-ones, in which five of the nine sales managers he supervised were brought to tears more than once, he heard repeatedly how his endless lectures and constant harangues during team meetings were debilitating and demotivating.

This branch manager also learned during his sessions that he was too quick in taking problems away from his subordinates and that he didn't spend enough time listening to them. "It makes us angry and frustrated when you take over and try to solve our problems for us," several of them told him. "Since you don't ask enough questions, you don't have nearly enough information to come up with good solutions. So now we come to you with a problem only when we really have to."

Management issues like these are common in organizations in change and often manifest themselves as B-1 or B-3 problems, especially with employees who are reluctant to confront a superior directly. Without the aid of the belief system approach, which promotes honest and open communication, employees will sometimes circumvent the real issue—their boss's unnerving or demoralizing behavior—by shouldering much of the responsibility for the problem themselves. "I don't think I have what it takes to succeed under this kind of pressure" (B-1), they might say, or "This is not the kind of work environment that really suits me" (B-3).

Using the belief system approach, however, sensitive issues relating to personality and behavioral style can be broached without fear, even when the feedback is not easy to deliver—or listen to. This was the case with the branch manager just described, who was so genuinely surprised at what his subordinates had to tell him that he was frequently overcome with emotion during the sessions he conducted. Though it was difficult for him to receive such unpleasant news over and over again, the commonalities among the comments he heard from his people convinced him that what they were saying was true and that he had to change his style in the future.

Matching Style to Employee Needs

In two other cases, branch managers also learned that their supervisory approach had to be modified, though the feedback they received from their subordinates was substantially different from that heard by the branch manager just discussed. These two branch managers had to become *more* decisive and directive, their people told them, and step in more frequently to provide help when it's needed during the change.

Both patient, considerate, and well liked, these leaders were accustomed to practicing a hands-off, "run your own shop" management style that might have worked effectively with accomplished sales managers who operate well independently. But the majority of sales managers did not fit this profile in either branch. On the contrary, a good number of them were former sales representatives who were new to management, who were finding it hard to deal with the change, and whose performance results were uneven.

Pervasive B-2 problems—the belief that outcomes are not tied to performance—were obstacles to improvement in both branches. Since these leaders were slow to take action whenever performance problems arose (i.e., to either discipline, fire, or provide extra help to subordinates), their sales managers tended to shrug off criticism and to ignore any warnings that their bosses might issue.

In both cases, the one-on-one sessions were a wake-up call for these branch managers that helped them realize that their management style was inappropriate for the people they were managing and that they had to adopt a different approach. Though one of these branch managers was more amenable to change than the other, both were able to draw up detailed To Do lists that headed them in the right direction, based on the information they received from subordinates during their one-on-ones.

Small Adjustments, Major Results

As these examples show, the belief system approach can help managers achieve a new level of self-awareness by educating them about the impact their working style has on subordinates. Many managers have no knowledge of how they affect others emotionally. Oftentimes, their management style has evolved over a period of years or even decades, and they've received little or no feedback about how it makes the people they supervise really feel.

What Employees Ask Their Managers to Do

"Offer more positive reinforcement."

"Don't yell and scream so much."

"Be available to spend time with us when we need you."

"Don't cut me off before I finish talking."

"Let me know what I'm doing right."

"Help me solve problems; don't solve them for me."

"Provide enough coaching and training."

"Don't lie to us."

"Be more decisive; don't procrastinate."

"Be more specific in explaining what you want."

During one-on-one sessions that focus on management style, it's not uncommon for managers to receive the same feedback from different subordinates: "Please don't yell and scream so much," "Try to be more specific in explaining what you want," or "Don't cut me off before I finish what I have to say." Many come away with the knowledge that if they could change just three or four aspects of the way they manage, their people would be more receptive to their direction and they would be significantly more effective as managers.

In the vast majority of cases, these sessions indicate that major behavioral changes are not required, and most managers are willing to make the stylistic adjustments that their subordinates say they need. Of course, there are always those few—even smart and confident managers—who feel threatened by any criticism from subordinates or refuse to change practices that they believe are intrinsic to their nature. But most managers are grateful for this kind of feedback and eager to take the steps that will help them to operate more effectively at work.

SOLVING CHANGE-RELATED PROBLEMS

Though discussions about management style are prevalent during one-on-ones, problems related to change almost always dominate these sessions when an organization applies the belief system approach during a transformation effort. This was true in the Eastern Region of Middle Markets, especially during the sessions conducted between branch managers and sales managers and between sales managers and their representatives.

Among sales managers, for example, one common change-related problem had to do with coaching, a critical but sensitive topic. In the new "performance culture" designed for Middle Markets, managers were expected to spend at least 40 percent of their time on this activity, coaching on average at least one sales call per day and providing direction for call preparation and selling strategy. But few of the sales managers actually did.

Sales Manager Time	
Executive selling:	< 30 percent
Managing Office and Staff:	< 30 percent
Coaching:	> 40 percent

"I don't have the time to coach," was the excuse most often given, but when pressed, many sales managers confessed that their real reason for neglecting this important responsibility had to do with either a lack of skill ("I'm really not good at coaching"), a B-1 problem, or a disinclination ("I just don't like to coach"), a B-3 problem. Though all sales managers were offered special training in coaching at the time that Middle Markets was launched, the one-on-one sessions revealed that additional training was often necessary, as well as increased reinforcement of the need and benefits of coaching.

Other change-related problems that came out in the sessions had to do with the length of the sales cycle, the new skills that had to be mastered in developing relationships with customers, and the proliferation of new products that AT&T was introducing to mid-size customers in its quest to remain competitive in the marketplace. In all three areas, sales managers and sales representatives were voicing significant B-1 concerns: The difficulties they were having in managing longer sales cycles were undermining their confidence and motivation, they told their bosses during one-on-ones. They didn't know how to successfully approach new customers and penetrate existing accounts, they said, which increased their feelings of frustration. And they often felt confused and overwhelmed by all the new and highly technical communications products they had to learn about.

But once these problems were clearly identified, both manager and employee were usually able to work together to determine their causes and come up with effective solutions. In many cases, additional skill development was the most appropriate remedy. Special training in time management, account development, or strategic selling, for example, was one important way that sales managers and reps could beef up their repertoire of selling skills and boost their confidence on sales calls. Or, to help them bone up on new products, a common solution was to invite technical experts from the corporate office to visit the branch and make special presentations.

Hard-to-Solve Problems

Naturally, not all the change-related problems that surfaced during the one-on-ones were amenable to easy solutions. Some problems extended into areas that were beyond the control of managers, while others could be solved only partially or temporarily. But even in these cases, having the opportunity to raise their concerns helped sales managers and representatives to feel better about their jobs and maintain their motivation.

Some of these hard-to-solve problems had to do with the Middle Markets compensation plan. Sales representatives often complained that the plan changed too frequently, raising and lowering quotas month by month on the different products that were offered and constantly creating new financial incentives. "It's hard for us to keep track of what we're supposed to sell," reps told their managers with annoyance. "Just when we get all fired up to sell a certain product, the comp plan suddenly changes and we have to refocus on something completely different."

Though there was little within their power that managers could do to alleviate this problem, the one-on-one sessions at least gave them the opportunity to explain the rationale behind alterations in the comp plan and to show how they related to competitive shifts and rapid changes in the marketplace. While this was not a solution to the problems voiced by their subordinates, it did help managers to smooth some ruffled feathers and promote greater understanding of the organization's strategic goals.

Similar types of problems surrounded the new sales reporting system that had been developed for Middle Markets. A common bugbear among salespeople, the requirement that they key in sales data for every client was onerous and time consuming, reps in the Eastern Region complained, and it took them away from revenue-producing activities. What's more, the system contained too many glitches (a common occurrence in start-up organizations), and didn't always work the way it was supposed to. Here, again, though managers didn't have the ability to solve these problems, the one-on-one sessions helped to make their subordinates feel better by allowing them to express their emotions and get these concerns off their chest.

Identifying Job Mismatches

In a number of one-on-one sessions conducted during the cascade, both manager and subordinate came to the conclusion that the best answer to the problems being voiced was for the subordinate to look for work elsewhere. Though the belief system approach doesn't encourage such separations, it usually involves such a thorough examination of what employees want from their job—and what managers expect from their people during a change—that this solution is often the most practical and realistic. In most cases, moreover, these separations are amicable and in the best interests of both parties.

One Eastern Region sales manager, for example, realized during a heated, nine-hour one-on-one session that her high-powered and aggressive operating style was too similar to her manager's and was the source of much of their ongoing conflict on the job. Though the two were able to establish ground rules during the session that allowed them to work together for some months more peacefully, the sales manager eventually decided that she would probably be better off working for another boss and voluntarily left the organization.

Cascading the belief system approach produced similar results in a number of other branches. In one case, the discussion conducted during a one-on-one session led the branch manager to shift one of the sales managers on his team to a staff position, a job more suited to her temperament and skills. In another branch, a sales manager resigned even before his one-on-one session took place. Just going through the two-day learning session and finding out what the belief system was all about, he later said, was enough to make him start thinking seriously about his job and realize that he wasn't cut out for it.

The most unusual example of a job mismatch had to do with a one-on-one session in which the subordinate, a sales manager, said that he was completely satisfied with his job and with the branch manager who supervised him. "I love my work, and everything is great," the sales manager told his boss, "and I can't think of a single thing that I want you to do differently." Since such feedback almost never occurs during a one-on-one session, especially when both parties are truly honest about how they feel, the branch manager became suspicious of this subordinate and began to scrutinize his performance more closely. Sure enough, he soon discovered a consistent pattern of deception on the part of the sales manager (who, as it turned out, inflated his sales results and consistently concealed performance problems), a situation that resulted in the sales manager's dismissal.

A FOCUS ON INDIVIDUAL NEEDS

No matter how minor or serious the problems that surfaced during the one-on-one sessions in the Eastern Region, applying the belief system approach helped managers work with their subordinates to effectively solve those problems and identify clearly what was needed to motivate their subordinates better. Managers gained a clearer understanding of how their people wanted to be managed and what each one needed in order to maintain optimal performance.

In many cases, the solutions they applied to employee problems were fairly obvious and straightforward: to provide formal training to improve selling skills, to coach more frequently to model critical skills, or to accompany sales representatives on more calls to instill confidence. These were often the types of solutions that were applied when salespeople voiced problems related to account development, account penetration, or closing enough calls to reach quota.

For instance, sales representatives in Middle Markets were expected not only to win new customers for AT&T and retain them as clients, but also to win back old customers who had been lost over the years to competitors. As a result, there were two quotas that had to be routinely met—one for "retention" and one for "win back"—but not all sales representatives were comfortable or skilled at doing both. Though this created significant B-1 problems ("Getting this customer to come back to us is a real uphill battle, and I'm not sure I can do it," salespeople would lament), solving them was fairly easy: Sales managers and representatives would collaborate more closely on sales planning and strategy, for example, or conduct more joint sales calls.

Customized Solutions

In other cases, managers and their subordinates had to come up with more creative solutions to motivation and performance problems, especially those that had to do with behavioral style or with teamwork. Here, solutions often had to be customized to the parties involved, and take into consideration their individual needs and unique capabilities.

One sales manager, for example, supervised a high-performing sales representative who suffered from severely strained relations with her peers and with the people in the branch who provided her with technical support. A hard-driving and aloof perfectionist, this representative had a working style that alienated many of the people she interacted with and led them to think that she didn't like them. To solve this problem, the manager and the representative agreed during their one-on-one session to move her desk to the center of the branch office. There, surrounded by many of the people she had problems with, she was forced to come into contact with them more often, get to know them on a personal level, and build more positive working relationships.

A similar case had to do with an overachieving sales representative who was so aggressive during sales calls that he started having arguments with some of his biggest customers. During his one-on-one session, his manager discovered that this behavior occurred mainly with customers who reminded the sales rep of his stepfather—an especially difficult-to-please and contentious parent—so the manager took some unusual steps. Whenever he assigned an account to this sales rep, he would first investigate the personality of the customer to avoid any potentially explosive situations. This strategy worked so well, the manager later related, that he eventually developed a ongoing system for matching salespeople with customers based on their personality styles.

The Motivating Power of Money

One of the most important lessons managers learned from their one-on-one sessions in the Eastern Region is that money is hardly ever an effective solution to performance problems, nor is it a primary motivator for employees. Though many people assume that increased salaries, higher bonuses, and ongoing financial incentives are vitally important to employees, this is not what managers normally hear when they conduct their one-on-ones.

In those organizations that apply the Belief System Profile (see Chapter 7), for example, employees are asked to rate their level of satisfaction with forty-nine motivators on a scale of -10 to +10. Though money is listed at the top of the page, rarely is it included among the items that employees rate the highest. "Of course, money is important to me," employees will tell their managers in the discussions evaluating their profile, "but it's not the *most* important thing to me."

What Motivates Employees Most?

It all depends. Though many managers would like to believe that the same motivators apply across the board—and that effective managers operate the same way with everyone—the truth is altogether different. Employees are individuals, and each one is motivated in a unique way.

Still, that doesn't mean that motivating employees is difficult. If you want to know what really motivates your employees, all you have to do is *ask!*

In just about every organization where the belief system approach is applied, money is almost never the response when employees are asked specifically what they need to perform better in their jobs or become more motivated. Though the answer to this question varies widely among employees, in the vast majority of cases it has to do with how they want to be managed by their boss. Some will say they need more encouragement and praise; others will ask for more performance feedback and coaching; still others want the opportunity to perform more meaningful work or earn the respect of their peers. For many, simply developing a strong and positive working relationship with their supervisor is enough to keep them highly motivated and satisfied at work.

Given this fact, why is it that so many organizations focus on money when they seek to improve motivation and performance? Though there's no clear answer to this question, one possible explanation is that the people who are hired to develop incentive programs are themselves motivated strongly by money, and they assume that others are too. Another explanation is that money incentives do work at times, but only in motivating those few for whom money is a top priority.

Many sales managers, for example, will insist on introducing one financial incentive program after another because, they claim, these programs always increase sales. But what these managers fail to realize is that the increase they gain can be attributed to the handful of salespeople who really want the money and are the most likely to win it, while the rest remain largely unaffected. Rarely do these managers stop to think how much more productive their sales force could be— or how much higher their sales revenues—if their people were motivated by the things they really want.[1]

BEGINNING AN EMOTIONAL TURNAROUND

By the end of 1995, the implementation of the belief system approach had begun to demonstrate favorable results throughout the Eastern Region. Many of the negative and potentially disruptive emotions that had characterized the launch of Middle Markets began to dissipate, and managers and their subordinates were beginning to enjoy more satisfying and more productive working relationships. Interviews conducted during this time indicated that an emotional turnaround had begun to take place in the Eastern Region of Middle Markets and that substantial progress was being made in coping with change.

"The belief system has had a tremendous impact in a lot of ways, most importantly on the relationships I have with my people," said one manager. "I learned that my style wasn't what they wanted, and they were reluctant to open up to me. But now they come to me more often, and we're ending 1995 on a more positive emotional note."

Another manager agreed that implementing the belief system was beneficial to the change effort and provided a mechanism that helped people to cope with change better. "Feedback from the one-on-one sessions taught me that I'm doing better than I thought," he said, "and that gave me more confidence in handling this change. It reassured me of the approaches I was taking, and I learned new tactics for solving problems."

In the following chapter, we'll examine other indicators to show the value of this approach to the success of Middle Markets and review the qualitative and quantitative measures that were used to evaluate its impact.

NOTE

1. Numerous studies have indicated that money is not a primary motivator among employees or an especially effective one. For example, in her book *Recognition, the Quality Way* (Quality Resources, New York, 1995), consultant Toni LaMotta presents the results of a survey she conducted showing that managers commonly mistake money as the number-one motivator, while employees are much more likely to ask for other forms of recognition. Among them are respect from the people they work with and the feeling that who they are and what they do at work really makes a difference.

13

Outcomes and Measured Results

When an organization achieves success through major change, it's not always possible to identify the factors that contributed most to improvement. But attempting to do so is critical if we are to understand how to implement change effectively and learn what it takes to bring about quantum leaps in productivity, quality, motivation, and performance.

Analyzing the success of Middle Markets is especially difficult because so many variables were involved in the change effort. At least a dozen discrete change-management initiatives were introduced to create the organization and establish a new sales culture. Innovative prospecting techniques were used, different selling skills were put into practice, and new ways of managing and rewarding performance were applied.

The fact that the organization was targeting a new and relatively unfamiliar customer base also complicates the analysis. What role, for example, did customer needs play in the overall performance of Middle Markets? Did the burgeoning list of mid-size customers assure hefty sales increases for AT&T no matter what changes were implemented? Or were some changes more critical than others to identifying the new buying behaviors and business needs of this untapped market?

To isolate the belief system approach among these many variables and attempt to assess its contribution would not be easy either. But since a great deal of time and energy had been invested in this improvement strategy, the Eastern Region leadership agreed that some effort must be made to measure its effectiveness. Consequently, a multipronged approach was developed to evaluate the impact of the approach, an assessment that would serve two purposes: It would help managers determine the importance of motivation improvement during change—and what must be done to promote improvement—and it would establish the value of the belief system to change efforts in other companies attempting large-scale transformations.

Three Assessment Methods

Several techniques were used to evaluate the approach. One involved conducting in-depth interviews with managers and sales representatives. Another was to administer leadership surveys before and after the implementation. A third, more indirect approach was to compare scores for the AT&T Opinion Survey (AOS), distributed yearly to all company employees, from 1994 to 1995.

In the end, the results from both surveys provided quantitative proof that the belief system had a significant and positive impact on the Eastern Region. Subordinate evaluations of their managers were substantially more favorable following implementation of the approach, and they demonstrated a stronger confidence in management. The comparison of AOS scores also showed a significant rise in employee satisfaction after implementation. Employees felt more empowered and motivated, had greater respect for their managers, and professed a stronger sense of dedication and teamwork.

Qualitative evaluations that were gathered through interviews revealed an almost universal endorsement of the approach from those who completed the four-part process (see Chapter 7). A common message among these interviews was that the belief system approach has the power to transform the negative emotions of change through dialogue and communication, and it improves working relationships. One sales representative, for example, claimed that implementing the approach was the catalyst that initiated a "100-percent turnaround" in his emotional health and well-being. "I went from feeling angry and misunderstood at work to feeling very pleased," he said. "I give more to my job now because I'm not so angry inside, and my performance is better."

IMPRESSIVE BOTTOM-LINE RESULTS

Though it may not be possible to determine exactly how much of the Eastern Region's success can be attributed to the belief system approach, one thing is clear: Despite a shaky start, exceptionally strong competition, and the emotional upheaval caused by change, the Eastern Region outperformed every other region during the first year of Middle Markets and achieved every major sales target established for the organization. The success of the region was especially notable in three critical areas:

New Account Sales

The Eastern Region ranked highest in new account sales revenues, achieving 139 percent of its 1995 objective, and was the only BCS region in which all branch offices reached both their new account and customer-retention targets. The region was also distinguished by the consistency of its success in this area. Starting out in first place, it maintained a commanding lead in new account acquisition in every week of every sales campaign—throughout all four quarters of 1995 and in forty-seven out of forty-seven reporting weeks.

Discount Rate

What makes these sales figures even more remarkable is the fact that they were achieved without major price discounts. The average discount rate for the region, in fact, was the lowest within BCS for all of 1995. This means that salespeople in the Eastern Region brought in more revenue dollars per sale than their peers elsewhere and were the least likely to compete on the basis of price. A sign of superior selling power, this statistic also indicates a highly motivated sales force and one that relies strongly on the effectiveness of its sales approach and skills to identify needs and overcome objections, to build mutually beneficial relationships, and to attain high levels of customer satisfaction.

Sales Efficiency

The Eastern Region also led BCS nationwide in another key area of performance quality: sales efficiency. Revenues per salesperson were at least 10-percent higher in the Eastern Region, while its staff-to-salesperson ratio was the lowest within Middle Markets.

What's the importance of these statistics? They show that salespeople in the Eastern Region had the skills or motivation to close more sales than salespeople in other regions and could work more independently, with less technical and administrative support. And they demonstrate that the intelligent use, not simply the amount, of sales resources is what's critical to improving performance and increased revenues.

QUANTITATIVE SURVEY RESULTS

As impressive as these sales results are, however, they do not provide definitive proof that the belief system approach was worth implementing or that it played a significant role in bringing about improved performance. Though they might lead to the reasonable conclusion that the approach probably did not impede the success of the Eastern Region, to determine the actual impact of this improvement process we have to look at other measurements that show a more direct connection with what happened in the Eastern Region during 1995.

Among the most important of these are the results of two leadership surveys that were conducted among branch managers and their teams immediately following the implementation. They show conclusively that the way branch managers were perceived by their teams changed significantly—and for the better—as a result of the belief system approach. In general, branch managers were found to be more attuned to the needs and preferences of their direct reports, more skilled at resolving performance problems, and better at adapting their management styles to the individual needs of their people.

Leadership Survey I

In the first survey, branch and sales managers were asked to respond to twenty-five statements describing their boss. Using phrases like "accurately identifies performance problems," and "effectively resolves employee problems," the survey asked respondents to indicate the extent to which their boss performed certain critical management activities by circling either "never," "rarely," "infrequently," "frequently," "usually," or "always." The survey was administered at the end of the two-day learning session and again after the one-on-one sessions within each team were completed. (For Sales Vice President Ray Butkus's team of branch managers, the survey was administered a third time, twelve months later.)

Though the degree of improvement demonstrated by this survey varied among the managers rated, Ray Butkus and every one of his branch managers showed some improvement as measured by the number who received "favorable" ratings from subordinates (that is, either "frequently," "usually," or "always"). In one case, a branch manager received favorable ratings from all his direct reports (a 100-percent favorable response) for only two of the twenty-five activities the first time the survey was administered. At the team meeting conducted three months later, the number of activities for which this manager received a favorable rating from all his team members jumped to seventeen!

Indicate the extent to which your manager does each of the following:

Aggregate Scores:	% favorable (2-day learning)	% favorable (team meeting)
1. Links performance and outcomes so that rewards are obtained when performance is achieved.	86	95 (+ 9)
2. Understands what employees desire when performance exceeds expectations.	67	90 (+23)
3. Recognizes employees for high productivity.	86	98 (+12)
4. Builds the skills of employees in order to raise their performance.	53	81 (+28)
5. Sets difficult, yet attainable performance goals.	88	91 (+ 3)
6. Motivates employees to achieve results.	70	88 (+18)
7. Provides desired outcomes for performance.	70	91 (+21)
8. Substitutes desired but unavailable rewards with others that are desirable to employees.	52	72 (+20)
9. Adapts management approach to the style of the employee.	45	77 (+32)
10. Effectively resolves employee problems.	75	97 (+22)
11. Quickly recognizes symptoms of performance problems.	69	81 (+12)
12. Accurately identifies performance problems.	73	84 (+11)
13. Uncovers the causes of performance problems.	56	68 (+12)
14. Involves employees in solving their own performance problems.	66	95 (+29)
15. Chooses appropriate solutions to address performance problems.	61	86 (+25)
16. Implements solutions to performance problems.	63	72 (+ 9)
17. Follows up on solutions to performance problems that are implemented.	58	74 (+16)
18. Recognizes when effort decreases.	80	83 (+ 3)
19. Deals with declines in employee satisfaction.	63	74 (+11)
20. Prevents undesirable consequences from occurring for high performers.	70	79 (+ 9)
21. Matches employee skills with the skill requirements of the job.	88	91 (+ 3)
22. Determines the skills levels of employees.	81	93 (+12)
23. Provides necessary tools to get the work done.	69	93 (+24)
24. Provides assignments that satisfy employees.	84	93 (+ 9)
25. Offsets undesirable outcomes with desirable ones.	63	84 (+21)
Average score:	69	85 (+16)

Aggregate scores for all branch managers show improvement across the board in every management area. Though the average favorable rating score for all twenty-five activities (i.e., the percentage of sales managers who rated their boss "favorably") increased from 69 percent to 85 percent the second time around, average favorable scores for some activities rose by close to 30 points. There were four management areas that showed the greatest improvement: adapting management style to employee preferences, involving employees in solving performance problems, raising employee skill levels to improve performance, and choosing appropriate solutions to address performance problems.

There's also some evidence to suggest that these gains were sustained long after the one-on-one sessions were completed. When the survey was first administered with Ray Butkus's team, for example, the Sales Vice President received a favorable rating on only one measure. When one-on-ones with his team were completed three months later, Ray's scores soared and remained high a full year later.

Leadership Effectiveness over Time
(Ray Butkus's Team of Branch Managers)

Before the Belief System

- 100% favorable response on one of twenty-five measures

After three months

- 100% favorable response on ten of twenty-five measures
- improvement shown on twenty-three of twenty-five measures

After fifteen months

- 100% favorable response on eight of twenty-five measures
- improvement shown on twenty of twenty-five measures

Leadership Survey II

Though this first leadership survey was based solely on subordinate perceptions of their managers, it clearly points to an improvement in management effectiveness following the one-on-one sessions and is corroborated by a second leadership survey administered at the time team meetings were conducted. In this survey, sales managers were asked to respond to eighteen statements that described their relationship with their boss and how it changed as a result of using the belief system approach.

Leadership Survey II

As a result of the belief system approach	% agree/strongly agree
1. My manager understands me better.	93
2. My manager treats me better.	73
3. My manager makes better decisions about me.	86
4. My manager adapts more to my style.	79
5. My manager is more effective with me.	80
6. My manager has more respect for me.	75
7. My manager and I communicate better.	88
8. My manager and I have a better relationship.	79
9. My manager and I are more open and honest with each other.	86
10. My manager and I work better together.	80
11. It is safer to say what I think to my manager.	82
12. I like my job better.	59
13. I am more confident in my future.	59
14. I am more motivated.	61
15. I am performing better.	64
16. This is a better place to work.	64
17. The belief system has been well worth the time I have invested in it.	88
18. The belief system has been a breakthrough experience for me.	61

Here again, survey results showed that implementing the belief system approach had a positive impact on working relationships and helped improve motivation and morale. For example, an overwhelming majority of the sales managers in the region—93 percent—agreed with the statement, "My manager understands me better." Some 88 percent said they communicate better with their manager, and 86 percent said that their manager "makes better decisions about me."

Sales managers' ratings of the belief system itself were also favorable. Nearly nine out of ten managers (88 percent) agreed, "The belief system has been well worth the time I have invested in it," and more than half (61 percent) said they felt the approach was a "breakthrough experience" for them personally. More than six out of ten (64 percent) of the sales managers said, "I am performing better as a result of the belief system."

Employee Opinion Survey

Results from the AT&T Employee Opinion Survey also provide evidence of increased employee satisfaction and morale. Though a direct, year-to-year comparison of AOS scores isn't possible (Middle Markets did not exist in 1994), some insight into the changes that took place in employee attitudes can be gained by comparing the 1995 AOS scores for the Eastern Region to the 1994 scores for Ray Butkus's previous BCS team members, many of whom stayed on to join him in the new organization.

This comparison points to an upward trend in all seventeen AOS categories, a comprehensive list of statements and questions posed to employees that cover a broad range of organizational issues, from "dedication to the customer" to "pay and benefits." Favorable ratings by employees increased most in the categories of "recognition," "performance management," and "management leadership," precisely those areas that the belief system has historically impacted the most.

AOS Results (Ray Butkus's Organization)

Category	Percentage "Favorable"	
	1994	1995
1. Management Leadership	27	49 (+22)
2. Respect	34	51 (+17)
3. Teamwork	53	65 (+12)
4. Dedication to the Customer	45	58 (+13)
5. Integrity	61	71 (+10)
6. Empowerment	37	50 (+13)
7. Quality Process	31	51 (+20)
8. Supervision	63	73 (+10)
9. Performance Management	44	59 (+15)
10. Job Satisfaction	68	76 (+ 8)
11. Recognition	47	67 (+20)
12. Pay and Benefits	54	57 (+ 3)
13. Employment Security	45	51 (+ 6)
14. Operating Efficiency	47	54 (+ 7)
15. Competitive Position	61	69 (+ 8)
16. Company Satisfaction	41	60 (+19)
17. Diversity	(insufficient data)	

In the category of "recognition," for example, 77 percent of the employees in the Eastern Region agreed with the statement, "People who do a good job are recognized for their efforts," an increase of 24 percentage points over 1994. In the "performance management" category, some 83 percent of employees said they "understand how the work expected of me relates to the goals and objectives of my business unit" (up 15 points), and 62 percent agreed with the statement, "My managers do a good job of stating organizational goals clearly" (up 26 points).

AT&T Employee Opinion Survey (Eastern Region)

	Percentage "Yes"	
	1994	1995
Are you satisfied with your job?	44%	65%
Do you understand the goals of your organization?	61%	80%
Are you encouraged to come up with solutions to work-related problems?	60%	71%
Do you understand how your performance is evaluated?	62%	78%

AOS questions that are designed to measure overall levels of job satisfaction also showed major gains. For example, when employees were asked to rate their satisfaction with AT&T at the time of the survey, two-thirds said they were either "satisfied" or "totally satisfied" with their company, a rise of 24 percentage points in one year. Responding to another question in that same category, 77 percent of Eastern Region employees said they would "recommend AT&T as a good place to work," up 21 points over 1994.

In total, the number of categories in which "favorable" ratings from employees accounted for at least 65 percent of all responses—a score considered "world-class" among corporate survey experts—increased from one in 1994 to six in 1995. The number of categories with a favorable rating score of 50 percent or more climbed from six to fifteen.

While these gains would be unusual in any year-to-year comparison of AOS scores, they're especially noteworthy given the changes that took place in the organization during 1995. At a time when employee morale and job satisfaction would be expected to decrease, AOS scores showed that employees actually felt better about their organization than they did before the change took place and more confident in the abilities of their managers to lead them.

Personal Evaluations

Other important evidence that implementing the belief system approach was worthwhile comes from in-depth interviews, conducted throughout 1995 and 1996, with those who participated directly in the process. In their own words, these sales representatives, sales managers, and branch managers described how the approach changed their work lives and the impact it had on their motivation and performance.

AOS Results before and after the Belief System

	Number of Categories	
Percentage favorable	**1994**	**1995**
70+	0 ⎫	3 ⎫
65–69	1 ⎪	3 ⎪
60–64	3 ⎬ 6	1 ⎬ 15
50–59	2 ⎭	8 ⎭
40–49	6 ⎫	1 ⎫
30–39	3 ⎪	0 ⎪
20–29	1 ⎬ 10	0 ⎬ 1
10–19	0 ⎪	0 ⎪
0–9	0 ⎭	0 ⎭

Many of these interviews emphasized the same major theme: how the belief system approach helped increase mutual understanding between managers and their direct reports, encouraged and improved two-way communication, and resulted in better working relationships. "I saw a tremendous and positive difference in my relationship with my manager as a result of our one-on-one session," one salesperson acknowledged. "She got to learn how I think and how to manage me better, and I found out exactly what she expects of me." Said another Eastern Region salesperson, "After our session, I felt my manager made a genuine effort to communicate with me the way I wanted her to. Above all, she started giving me more feedback, which is important to me."

Sales and branch managers made similar comments, pointing to the power of the approach to ease stress and tension at work and convert troubled relationships into more productive ones. "The belief system has actually helped to save some critical relationships in our branch," said one sales manager. "A few people just weren't getting along with our boss, and the fallout was felt throughout our office. But now those relationships have improved, and we're functioning better as a group."

Another sales manager claimed that the approach was instrumental in transforming the highly competitive relationship she maintained with her boss into one that was more collaborative and comfortable: "I've always been competitive with the people who managed me, but I never realized before how much tension that brings to a working relationship. With this approach I got the chance to get a lot off my chest and say things I never said before, and that's made me feel better about coming into work here."

What Salespeople Said

"It gave me the opportunity to identify areas I needed to
    work on and reinforced my confidence in my manager."

"It forced me to sit back and listen more, and gave me a
    clearer definition of who I am."

"It helped me to map things out and get issues clear in my
    head, and gave me something concrete to work on."

"The whole process touched me spiritually, and made me
    think about the things that mattered most to me."

For branch managers, the chief benefits of the belief system included the new climate of teamwork and cooperation that it helped create and its power to build trust, a critical factor in organizational success that often breaks down during change. "On an interpersonal level, the impact of the approach was remarkable, but it was the way it changed us as a group that really made a difference," explained one branch manager. "After we went through the process, there were fewer personal attacks around here, more requests for opinions and solutions, and better feedback from subordinates. In general, there was a greater feeling of trust and more interest in helping the team succeed."

Another branch manager credited the belief system for improving his team's ability to diagnose and solve work problems. But even more important, he said, was the impact it had on how his team members interacted with each other. "Now my people seem more comfortable and open in asking for what they need, and we show more respect for one another," he said. By setting the stage for "productive discussions about what really matters," he added, the belief system helped his people to develop a better acceptance for other points of view and function more effectively as a team.

Emotional Catharsis

One of the most important ways the belief system helped to improve communication, these interviews suggested, was by allowing many underlying and negative emotions to surface and be expressed. Though the process of revealing their innermost feelings was often uncomfortable for people, most agreed with hindsight that it was a critical prerequisite to improved understanding and that there were important benefits to clearing the air emotionally. Said one salesperson, "Before meeting with my manager I was nervous and afraid of opening up. But I figured that the only way to make the session work was to be totally honest, so I decided to share how bad I really felt. It was good to finally identify those emotions and get them out in the open."

Though not every one-on-one session produces an emotional catharsis for participants, there are many examples from the Eastern Region where the venting of powerful emotions proved to be a critical turning point for managers and subordinates and permanently changed the nature of their relationship. One such case involved a top-performing salesperson who preferred to work at home, despite her manager's requests to show up at the office regularly, and resented any infringement on her independence and autonomy. "When I was preparing for my one-on-one session," this salesperson said, "some of the questions I was asked to consider made me so angry and bitter that I had tears in my eyes, and I came into the meeting ready for a fight. But afterward my happiness quotient went way up. By expressing how I truly felt, my manager got to know where I was coming from and what was really important to me. And I learned that performance isn't just sales—you sometimes have to meet political expectations." Though this salesperson admitted that antagonistic feelings toward her boss sometimes reappeared after their session, "I would catch myself and not let them happen, and our relationship definitely improved."

Even among those who got along well with their managers, there were many who said that their relationship became even better and was brought to a new level of mutual understanding and respect. This was the case with one of the organization's most successful salespeople, a twenty-eight-year-old woman with exceptional intelligence and drive, who said it became much easier for her to communicate with her boss—on both a personal and professional level—following a healthy expression of emotions during their one-on-one session. "At first, I was apprehensive about opening up because I'm the type of person who keeps things close to my chest," she said. "I was afraid that if I were really honest, it would have an adverse impact on our relationship. But sharing my feelings has actually made us much closer. Before the session, I used to talk to her only about business matters, but now I tell her all my frustrations and concerns because I know that she really cares." Being able to talk to her boss frankly, she said, also allowed her to speak more freely about the change and the impact it was having on her and on others. "Before our session I wouldn't talk about the transformation because I didn't want to come across as a whiner," she added. "But afterward I felt I could discuss it openly."

Many other participants described a similar development as a result of their one-on-one session: Following the honest exchange of feelings between manager and subordinate, these interview subjects

What Sales Managers Said

"It helped me to understand my people as individuals and tailor the way I work with them."

"I learned what really motivates me and have a better understanding of what it takes for me to change."

"I know my people better as a result of the belief system and how to approach them about change."

"I learned more about myself when I did the belief system with my team than when I did it with my boss. There is nothing more important I could have done."

claimed, communication between the two improved dramatically—and got better over time. "When you're able to tell your boss all your fears and not worry about it being used against you, that's really something," one sales manager said. "To this day, I feel that the one-on-one session I had with my boss was one of the best manager–subordinate discussions I've ever experienced—there was nothing that wasn't put on the table. And it changed the way we've related to each other ever since."

What Branch Managers Said

"It's given me greater insight into what motivates the members of my team, and they seem more at ease with me."

"I feel more in control and upbeat because of the belief system, and our results are more consistent across the board."

"It's increased our willingness to accept different styles and approaches, and people seem more patient with each other."

"It's given us a common language and helped us resolve some significant problems that were lingering."

Improved Confidence and Motivation

By helping people to recognize, cope with, and resolve any negative or troubling emotions, the belief system increased confidence and motivation in the Eastern Region. And that, many interview subjects indicated, led to better performance and increased sales. "It wasn't until my one-on-one session that I was able to go out and actually get a signed contract," said a new salesperson who had previously worked in technical support. "My confidence level went up, and I got a lot more help from my boss as a result of our one-on-one."

Though interview subjects offered a variety of explanations for their improved performance, one of the most commonly cited was the increased attention they received from their manager. "What impressed me the most about the approach was that it showed that my manager was concerned about me and was committed to learning how I operate," said one salesperson. "That gave me the motivation to prove that I was worth her time and concern for me."

A salesperson with a long history of conflict with her boss said that her level of motivation improved in part because the belief system helped resolve lingering but unstated issues she had with her manager and clarified performance expectations. But the way it contributed most to her motivation, she emphasized, was by showing that her manager really cared about her. "My biggest problem going into our session was that I didn't think she appreciated me, and afterwards I felt that she did," this salesperson said. "Being valued is an important issue for me. And the fact that she took the time to get to know me better helped me to realize that I wasn't just a faceless set of numbers to her, and I became more motivated."

For many in the region, these feelings of increased appreciation helped to generate closer working relationships and more collaboration between managers and subordinates, which translated into better bottom-line results. "Going through the process made me less reluctant to get my manager involved in what I was working on, and that's helped me to perform better," one salesperson said. "I got tremendous help from my manager as a result of our one-on-one session," said a salesperson who had been on the job for three months before participating in the process. "It just seemed like she wanted to help me more."

Another salesperson said that he and his manager now have more productive discussions about sales strategies and how to approach clients and that he feels better prepared when he goes out on calls to meet customers. A similar comment was made by a seasoned BCS manager, who said that the "bonding" that resulted from applying the approach helped her to become a better coach for her people and more effective at providing direction. "It's a lot easier to coach people when they know where you're coming from," she explained.

Many said they also developed better relationships outside the workplace—especially with customers—which has had a positive impact on their performance and results. "When I didn't understand customers before, I used to dismiss what they said and didn't bother to sell to them," said a salesperson who was new to AT&T. "But after having gone through the belief system process I find that I'm a better listener now. I work harder at trying to understand my customers and adapt to their style, and that's made me a better salesperson." An interview subject who admitted to having serious problems meeting her monthly sales quotas said that the belief system helped her become "more confident and comfortable with customers." "Even the relationships I have with the people who are close to me personally have changed for the better," she added.

Why does the belief system have this effect? One salesperson in the Eastern Region provided this succinct analysis: "Ultimately the entire process brings you to a new level of consciousness," he maintained. "You're so much more aware of yourself, your teammates, and your customers that you're operating in a totally different way." Another salesperson said it gives you a greater sense of confidence in dealing with difficult work situations—like organizational change—just by offering an effective process to help you cope better. "I'm much more willing to adapt and change now because I know I can handle the additional pressures," he said.

In the following chapter, we'll examine theoretical considerations to explain why the belief system approach delivers these benefits and offer additional insights into the results achieved by the Eastern Region.

PART V

RECOMMENDATIONS FOR SUCCESSFUL CHANGE

14

A Formula for Managing Change

"Overwhelmed." In a single word, that was how one new sales manager in BCS described his mental state just after the launch of Middle Markets in January 1995. A former product manager who had served briefly as a sales representative in the 1980s, he had just relocated his family to another city when he started his new career in the Eastern Region and was living with his in-laws while he looked for a home for his wife and children.

While these problems of transition and adjustment would be difficult for anyone to tackle, they were minor compared to the problems this manager faced with what he called his "other family": the members of his sales team. "They were like a bunch of kids in those days," he recalled during an interview. "They made so many phone calls to my home after hours that I was having a tough time separating my personal life from my professional one." Though the situation afforded him the opportunity to look good by "turning a bad situation into a good one," he said, he didn't anticipate "just how big the challenge would be" or how much time and attention his new team would require.

Over the coming months, this manager would rely heavily on the belief system approach to help him understand his people better—how they felt about the change and what problems they faced—and to provide the resources and solutions they needed to cope during the transformation. Throughout the year, he would apply the approach routinely in meetings with subordinates, to "crack issues" as they arose and ensure that goals were identified and met, and to ferret out stumbling blocks to productivity and performance for each member of his team.

With one salesperson who threatened to quit early on, for example, this sales manager was able to uncover the true causes of the dissatisfaction and to come up with an effective solution that would keep him on the job and happy. "When he told me that he didn't like his work because he wasn't making enough money, I assumed at first that we were dealing with a B-3 problem," the sales manager recalled. "But careful probing revealed that there were major B-1 issues involved, and that additional training and coaching was needed."

"The belief system approach has proved to be a tremendous tool for me as a manager," he asserted. "It's allowed us to break through emotions and solve problems rationally, and provided a clear understanding of what it is that drives each person on my team."

Change and Individuals

Together with the surveys and other interviews conducted during the first two years of Middle Markets, this manager's testimony affirms the value of the belief system approach and provides further evidence that it contributed to the impressive performance of the Eastern Region. But it also serves to demonstrate another important point: The success of organizational transformations depends largely on individuals—how they respond and adapt to change and how motivated they are to achieve their organization's new goals. This intimate connection between individuals and organizational change is not accidental, nor is it unique to the Middle Markets experience. As a formula for successful change, in fact, we believe that it holds true in all organizations and that the following principle consistently applies:

An organization's ability to change is directly proportional to the attention it pays to each individual's motivation to change.

Organizational change will fail, in other words, unless it focuses strongly on individuals and their motivation to change, and on their emotions—the feelings and beliefs that accompany change and that must be managed throughout the change process. Only in this way can organizations bring about the change of heart and change of mind that is required to implement change successfully.

This is the primary reason why we believe that the belief system approach is such an effective management tool: *It helps organizations to focus on each employee whenever they attempt to change.* Markedly different from other change-management approaches, this approach assumes that employees react to change in unique ways and helps managers to develop individual solutions to motivation and performance problems during change. What's more, it relieves managers of the burden of solving these problems on their own. It recognizes that employees know more about their motivation and performance than anyone else, and it involves them as partners in solving their problems at work.

THEORY BEHIND THE PRACTICE

The BCS case study presented in Part IV provides solid evidence that the belief system played a significant and positive role in the launch of Middle Markets. But how do we know that this approach is an effective management tool for every organization during change? One way is by examining its internal logic and philosophical soundness. Though practical management experience contributed substantially to the development of the belief system and its application in organizations, the model also rests firmly on a strong theoretical foundation that helps to explain its validity and effectiveness.

There are five basic principles that support the belief system change model. In this chapter, we'll examine each principle individually, analyze the requirements they establish for successful change management, and show how applying the belief system approach helps managers to meet these requirements in organizations that undertake change.

Principle 1

An organization's ability to change is greatest when it helps each individual to understand the organizational imperative to change.

Employees cannot be expected to understand on their own why their organization must change, nor can they be expected to understand clearly the business consequences of not changing. It is management's responsibility to create understanding and to convince employees to accept the imperative to change.

Most organizations realize the importance of communicating the change imperative, and many devote considerable resources to drafting communications for this purpose early on in their change effort. But most fail to drive home the message they must impart because their communication process works only one way. They fail to understand that telling is not enough. Employees don't always listen when the message represents change, and the message that is sent is not always received.[1] What's more, when the message to be communicated contains emotional content, it's not enough to communicate through memos, newsletters, or meetings. While written communications and group discussions serve an important purpose in facilitating change, they cannot substitute for interpersonal communication, which is essential.

Another reason why traditional communication efforts have a limited impact is that they frequently lose momentum once the change process gets under way. When the Principal Financial Group reengineered its Individual Insurance Department in the early 1990s, for example, a Communications Action Team was set up, special newsletters and reports were distributed, and "town meetings" were conducted during lunch hours to give employees a chance to pose questions and raise concerns. But over time the organization's leaders became sidetracked by the more immediate problems they faced, and they became less diligent at sustaining the dialogue that they had initially envisioned.[2]

How the Belief System Helps

The belief system approach helps managers communicate the imperative to change because it relies on two-way communication in a one-on-one format. When the imperative to change is not clearly understood by an employee, the approach allows for further clarification to ensure understanding and acceptance, and it creates a safe environment for emotional reactions to change to be expressed and dealt with.

The approach also helps ensure that the right message about change gets across to employees by creating a structured discussion around the organizational imperative to change. It gives managers the maximum opportunity to carefully prepare and accurately convey the change message, and it gives employees the opportunity to ask questions about, explore, and understand what they hear. Having a trained facilitator present during this discussion also ensures that the right message is both delivered and received.

Principle 2

An organization's ability to change is greatest when it helps each individual to understand the personal imperative to change.

Employees are more committed to change when they understand what it will mean for them personally and how it will affect their individual situation. Just as important, they must understand what will happen to them if they don't change and the consequences of adhering to outdated or ineffective work practices. The idea is to help them to see that changing will lead to certain outcomes (a B-2 issue) and to assess how they will feel about those outcomes once they come to pass (a B-3 issue).

Most organizations, however, are unable to frame the change message in a way that has personal meaning for employees. Whenever they attempt to address employee concerns, their change messages typically focus on general issues—not real or specific ones—because they don't understand what each employee expects or wants from the change. In addition, these messages tend to be highly selective in the information they provide, for fear that full disclosure will confuse employees or increase their apprehensions about what might happen to them in the future.

Change-management expert Dolorese Ambrose says that incomplete communications like these end up frustrating employees and alienating them from the change process. When employees feel that they're not getting the full picture, she says, they simply assume that their leaders are uncertain about the future (and don't really know what they're doing) or that the impact of the change on them will most likely be negative. Delivering these messages through one-way communications, with little opportunity for dialogue or feedback from employees, simply aggravates the situation, she says. Employees get the feeling that they're expected to "listen up" and do as they're told and that any personal concerns they may have don't really matter.[3]

It's important to remember that employees who lack a full understanding of what change will mean for them tend to "fill the gaps" in their knowledge with rumor and speculation. Left on their own to imagine how the change will affect them, they typically play out the worst possible scenarios in their minds. In an age when "organizational change" is so often associated with downsizings and layoffs, employees are likely to remain pessimistic about its impact, especially when the personal ramifications of change are not clearly spelled out.

How the Belief System Helps

The belief system approach promotes a stronger commitment to change because it works to define the personal imperative to change for each employee. Using a structured approach to help employees determine what they want from their job and how satisfied they are with what they're doing, it allows them to interpret the change effort within the context of their own expectations and aspirations. And by clearly outlining the consequences of changing versus not changing, the approach helps employees decide whether the change will be worthwhile for them and whether they can commit themselves fully to making it happen.

By focusing on the relationship between managers and their direct reports, the approach also helps employees to understand what the change will mean for their team (not just to their organization or company), which often defines the personal imperative to change. In many cases, employees cannot commit themselves fully to organizational change until they understand clearly how the work unit they relate to most strongly will be affected by it: how their team's membership will be modified, how new responsibilities will be allocated, or how reporting relationships will be redefined.

Achieving this clarity is essential to overcoming resistance to change, because it helps to eliminate many fears and uncertainties and promotes increased motivation. When employees are made aware of the consequences of change, they usually feel better about their jobs should they decide to stay on during the transformation. Though this knowledge may precipitate an initial "shake-up" when those who cannot accept the change decide to transfer or leave, it ultimately benefits organizations by allowing them to shed employees who might impede or slow down the change effort and retain those who can commit themselves wholeheartedly to it.

This may, in fact, have been what happened in the Eastern Region of Middle Markets during the year the belief system was implemented. Though turnover in that organization reached 35 percent in the twelve months following the launch—much higher than the average for most sales organizations—surveys showed that motivation and commitment among those who remained improved substantially (see Chapter 13). While high turnover often undermines motivation, in this case it was instrumental to creating a workforce that understood and accepted change and was committed to making it succeed.

Principle 3

An organization's ability to change is greatest when it helps each individual to understand how he or she is expected to change.

Most employees do not have the scope of understanding to translate the overall change strategy into an individual plan of action. Though many organizations work hard to communicate their change strategy and outline new objectives to employees, they usually do too little to help their employees understand how they must change as individuals.

Organizations cannot expect their employees to change without guidance or direction. They can't just say "do it" and hope that employees will know how they should act in the future or what they should do differently to promote their new goals. Nor is it appropriate for managers to decide unilaterally how employees have to change. Though managers play a strong role in making this decision, employees must have a voice in designing their own futures.

By participating in making change-related decisions concerning their jobs, employees are more likely to stay motivated during the change effort and to develop the skills and abilities that will improve organizational performance. Three skill areas for employees are typically affected by organizational change:

1. *Technical skills.* As more organizations modernize their operations to improve efficiency and customer service, employees must master new technologies and computer systems.
2. *Interpersonal skills.* As more organizations adopt team-based structures, employees must develop the ability to work effectively in groups and adjust to new routines that require them to work closely with others.
3. *Management skills.* As organizations become leaner and push down decision-making responsibilities, employees must learn critical management skills, such as problem solving, project planning, priority setting, and quality control.

How the Belief System Helps

The belief system approach provides the structure for determining how each individual is expected to change and promotes cooperation in making change-related decisions that affect the individual. The first way it does this is by requiring managers to participate in one-on-one discussions with *their* managers. This helps them to understand clearly how the change will affect their jobs, the impact it will have on their unit or team, and what it will mean to each individual they support. Equipped with this knowledge, managers can then work closely with their subordinates to determine exactly how job responsibilities will change and what will be required from each employee that is new or different.

The belief system also requires managers and their direct reports to identify expectations for change when preparing for their one-on-one session and then, in the presence of a trained facilitator, to work jointly to establish a plan the employee can follow to meet those expectations. If the expectations for individual change are not realistic, the two can work together to determine what resources (training, coaching, etc.) the employee will need to succeed on the job. If these expectations cannot be met even with additional support, the two may decide that the employee should leave the organization and look for work elsewhere. In either case, important decisions regarding the individual's ability to change are made early in the change effort and collaboratively.

This process of translating organizational goals into individual action plans may seem like a necessary precondition for any change initiative. But it doesn't always take place in organizations, and rarely does it focus on each individual. Even in Middle Markets, where extensive planning and communication efforts were conducted to prepare for change, employees did not always feel secure in the knowledge of what they were expected to do. As one manager recalled in a recent interview, "Before we started using the belief system approach, I never really sat down with my boss to learn what I needed to know for my job, to get oriented in the new organization, and to learn what he expected from me. And there was nobody else I could turn to for help."

Principle 4

An organization's ability to change is greatest when it determines and strengthens each individual's motivation to change.

Organizations recognize the importance of motivation during change and, to improve it, often set up new compensation systems or incentive programs whenever they initiate large-scale change. But rarely do they ask this critical question: What are the barriers to motivation? Even more infrequent is the attempt to answer this question for each employee. Most organizations assume that all employees are motivated by the same things when, in fact, motivation is highly unique to individuals, and what motivates one employee may have little or no impact on the motivation of another—or may even have a negative impact. An all-expenses-paid vacation in Hawaii, for example, is not an attractive reward for an employee who needs a bigger paycheck to finance a child's education. For another employee, however, getting such a raise might mean relatively little, especially if praise and recognition are more potent motivators. Though the list of potential motivators is infinite, most organizations focus only on the "big three": money, promotions, and job security. These rewards are definitely desired by some employees, but they do not satisfy everyone, nor do they compensate when other preferred rewards are lacking. As a result, organizations often miss significant opportunities to improve motivation because they fail to determine what it is that their employees really want.

This failure stems from another mistake organizations commonly make: assuming that motivation improvement is exclusively a management responsibility. Because managers are so often expected to address and overcome resistance to change on their own—with no organizational support or input from subordinates—it's no wonder that they consistently misjudge what employees want for doing a good job and rarely achieve optimal levels of motivation and performance.

How the Belief System Helps

The belief system approach to motivation improvement is totally different. First, it encourages managers to understand what it is that motivates each and every one of their employees. Second, it encourages managers and their direct reports to share the responsibility for dealing with motivation and performance problems. With this approach, managers apply the strategy, "If you want to know, ask": If you want to know what the problem is, ask the person who has the problem; if you want to know what the cause of the problem is, ask; if you want to know the solution, ask. Naturally, employees are reluctant to step forward and volunteer this kind of information to their managers. But we have found over the years that they are more than willing to talk about such issues if they are asked to do so.

Because it relies on structured, facilitated discussions, the belief system approach allows managers to get help in improving motivation and performance and allows employees to give help. These discussions encourage employees to "open up" to their manager in order to (1) identify any motivation or performance problems they're having relative to the change (B-1, B-2, or B-3 problems) and (2) assist in identifying causes and solutions that will work. The one-on-one sessions enable a "working together" to determine and strengthen each individual's motivation to change.

When we asked one experienced manager in Middle Markets about the impact these sessions had on her team, she answered, "There was nothing more important that I could have done as a manager." The sessions helped her to recognize how different her team members are from each other, she said, and discover what it takes to motivate each one individually. "Before, I used to treat everybody the same. It was part of my style to set high expectations and be demanding," she said. "But now I focus on understanding each person and learning what each one needs in order to stay motivated."

Principle 5

An organization's ability to change is greatest when it focuses first on each manager's motivation to change.

Many organizations fail to recognize the motivation problems that exist among managers during change. They assume their managers fully support the change effort and that they're willing to do whatever is needed to ensure the success of change. But many managers are thrown off balance when change takes place and don't feel equipped to handle it effectively. They may doubt their ability to operate in a changed environment (a B-1 problem), believe they can get by without changing (a B-2 problem), or dislike the work they'll be expected to do as a result of change (a B-3 problem). What's more, many managers don't have the skills or abilities to cope with how change will affect their subordinates (B-1). Consequently, they ignore the emotional impact that change has on their people and try to function without the support and commitment that change requires. Or they operate in denial, deluding themselves into thinking that motivation and morale will return once employees pass through an interim period of confusion and insecurity.

The reality is that organizations have an enormous amount to lose when managers aren't motivated to change. As leaders of change, managers play a critical role in helping others to understand it—why it's necessary and how it will help—and in modeling the new behaviors that change will require.[4] Managers also shepherd their subordinates through the change process. They provide training and coaching when needed, inspire others to meet the challenges of change, and act as a sounding board for complaints and concerns. When management motivation is lacking, these functions are performed poorly or not at all, and organizational transformations suffer. Employees doubt the necessity and legitimacy of change, they resist learning new skills, and they question the willingness and ability of management to take care of their needs. Without leaders who are fully committed to change, organizations cannot manage the trauma of transformation or help their employees develop the motivation and stamina to survive it successfully.

How the Belief System Helps

The belief system approach recognizes that managers who are expected to lead change often lack motivation themselves. That is why it focuses on managers as well as employees, and works to identify and resolve the issues that weaken management motivation.

Cascading assures that both managers and employees benefit equally from the approach and that managers are committed—in their hearts and minds—to the change effort before they address the problems of their subordinates (see Chapter 7). Cascading helps organizations to deal swiftly with managers who are unable to change, and it clarifies roles and expectations for those who want to stay on. "The belief system didn't just happen to my people, it happened to me," one manager in the Eastern Region said. "I learned what motivates me and have a better understanding of what it takes for me to change."

Managers and Motivation

"The one-on-one helped me to map out things and get issues clear in my head. It gave me something concrete to work on."

"This approach helped me to adjust to change and the pressures involved. Now I'm more willing to adapt and change."

"As a result of using this approach, I feel more in control, upbeat, and less disenfranchised from my team."

"I feel that the one-on-one was one of the most valuable discussions I ever had with my manager. I felt very positive about it—that we could change and become better."

Most important, the belief system provides managers with an effective tool that they can use to guide, direct, and motivate subordinates more effectively during periods of change. With a structured, proven approach to managing the emotions of change, managers are more confident in their ability to lead change and better able to handle the unique motivation and performance problems that arise as a result of it.

An organization's ability to change is greatest when it

- helps each individual to understand the organizational imperative to change.
- helps each individual to understand the personal imperative to change.
- helps each individual to understand how he or she is expected to change.
- determines and strengthens each individual's motivation to change.
- focuses first on each manager's motivation to change.

CONCLUSION

Examining the belief system from this theoretical perspective may help you to understand why this approach works better than other change-management strategies and why it increases the probability for successful change. In our last chapter, we'll look at this approach more practically. We'll examine the change-management lessons learned by BCS in the launch of Middle Markets, and we'll offer hands-on advice on how to apply the belief system approach for optimal results in your organization.

NOTES

1. Organizational behavior expert Robert Quinn claims that managers typically rely on one of two strategies to communicate change: telling and coercing. When changes are small and to the liking of employees, the telling strategy may work, says Quinn, but it usually fails when the changes involved are substantial. In those situations, managers often turn to coercion, attempting to induce change by issuing some kind of warning or threat. "Like a criminal with a pointed gun," says Quinn, "we can get, for a short while, the behavior change we desire, but it is unlikely to last, and the long-term relationship tends to be damaged." See Robert E. Quinn, *Deep Change: Discovering the Leader Within* (San Francisco: Jossey-Bass, 1996).

2. In an article evaluating this reengineering effort, Principal Executive Vice President Charles Rohm suggests that a more effective communication strategy might have helped employees to cope better with the emotional aspects of change. He writes, "Reengineering is an evolutionary process that often means working through long periods of ambiguity and uncertainty. To help people live with the unknown—and to dispel unwarranted fears—constant communication is absolutely essential." For more information, see "The Principal Insures a Better Future by Reengineering Its Individual Insurance Department," *National Productivity Review* 12 (Winter 1992–1993): 55–64.

3. For further information, see Dolorese Ambrose, *Healing the Downsized Organization* (New York: Harmony Books, 1996).

4. Managers' ability to "walk the talk" is critical to the success of organizational change, says Dolorese Ambrose in *Healing the Downsized Organization*:

The goal of the manager–leader is to align employees so that everyone is moving in the direction of change. Communication becomes a key part of the equation. Through constant, open communication, manager–leaders must explain the present state accurately and honestly. They must then articulate the vision in a convincing, engaging manner and describe the ideal end state so that people want to go there and know the criteria for assessing whether they have arrived. They must communicate value and goals, but more importantly they must model the way. (73)

15

Twelve Change-Management Lessons

Organizations require the best from their people during times of change. In order to succeed at renewal and achieve their change imperative—as well as the market competitiveness, customer focus, and streamlined organizational structures that they want—a committed workforce isn't just desirable, it's essential.

All too often this requirement isn't met. Hoping their people will be excited by change, organizations in transition frequently encounter the opposite reaction: resistance from employees, diminished motivation, and a reluctance to participate actively to make the change succeed. Instead of giving their best, people working in organizations undergoing change typically function at reduced levels of performance, and sometimes at their worst.

Though this reaction is unwanted and usually unplanned for, it's not uncommon. In many cases, it can be traced to the emotional discomfort that accompanies change and to the fears, anxieties, and insecurities that arise in people whenever organizations attempt to change. Leaders who are charged with managing change, therefore, must recognize this fact: Change produces powerful emotions that can undermine resolve and weaken motivation. If organizations want to succeed at change, they must learn how to manage these emotions effectively, and from the very start.

As the leaders in the Eastern Region of AT&T's Business Communications Services division recognized, relying solely on new work systems and organizational structures to ensure change can be a recipe for disaster. To implement change successfully, it's necessary to win employees' hearts, as well as their minds. This requires a greater sensitivity on the part of managers and the willingness of employees to acknowledge their problems and to work through them. But managers and employees cannot be expected to adopt these attitudes on their own. Solid organizational support is essential, and this support can be provided through change-management tools like the belief system of motivation and performance.

Focusing on Execution

As with any improvement strategy, the effectiveness of the belief system depends strongly on how it's carried out. It's not enough to embrace the concepts and objectives of the approach. Execution is critical. For when the belief system is applied consistently and throughout an organization in change, managers and employees report real breakthroughs in achieving new levels of motivation and performance. These results can be sustained if the approach is fully integrated into the organization and becomes a new way of managing and solving problems.

What was learned from the Eastern Region experience? And how can the belief system be implemented for maximum effectiveness elsewhere? In this chapter, we'll examine some insights gained by the leaders of the Eastern Region and offer advice to other organizations that are considering this change-management tool.

The Belief System Change Model

Theory

For people to be highly motivated during change, they
    must believe

"I can do it."

"Outcomes will be tied to my performance."

"Outcomes will be satisfying to me."

Application: Apply tools to

diagnose change-related motivation and performance
    problems

establish the causes of the problems

agree on solutions to the problems

Implementation
two-day training session
one-on-one session
team meeting
follow-up sessions every six months

STRATEGIES FOR SUCCESSFUL IMPLEMENTATION

After conducting an in-depth review of how change was implemented in the Eastern Region and what could have been done differently, we compiled this list of twelve change-management lessons.

Lesson 1

Establish the optimal time for implementation.

When we conducted interviews with managers in the Eastern Region, we posed this question: "When is the best time to introduce the belief system to an organization in transition?" The responses we received were wide-ranging. Some managers said that it was "never too early" to implement the approach; others said that one-on-one sessions should begin at the same time that changes take place; still others felt that a breathing period should be allowed before the approach is initiated. One manager said, "If you introduce the belief system too early, it may not be as helpful because people are focused on extrinsic things, and problems haven't surfaced yet. But if you wait too long the problems will fester and become worse than they should."

While there are no hard-and-fast rules that apply to timing with this approach, it may be wise to heed this manager's advice, especially when organizational change is conducted on a large scale and relatively quickly. The reason is that introducing the belief system to managers and employees who must cope with massive change "overnight" may exacerbate their feelings of being overwhelmed and prevent them from giving the approach the attention it requires. As in the case of the Eastern Region, when a totally new organization was created with a different structure and culture, people need time to size up their new work environment before they can identify and deal with their emotional reactions to it.

When changes to an organization are introduced gradually, however, the question of timing may not be as critical. But even in these cases, implementing the belief system should be delayed until after major change decisions have been finalized. For example, if you're planning to reengineer, make sure that new job designs and work flows have been established before starting to conduct your one-on-one sessions. Otherwise, the sessions will focus on what people *imagine* the change will entail, rather than on their emotional reactions to what is really happening.

Lesson 2

Maximize your benefits through increased participation.

When the belief system was first introduced to the Eastern Region of Middle Markets, branch and sales managers were allowed to decide on their own whether they wanted to apply it within their individual teams. The rationale for proceeding this way was based on a long-held respect for management autonomy within BCS and on the idea that you can't force medicine on an unwilling patient. When managers who resist the approach are required to implement it, there are any number of ways they can find to work around or undermine it.

Given this reality, however, leaders should strive to increase participation in order to maximize results, and winning over resistant managers may be one of the steps along the way. Why bother with managers who see no value in this approach? Because in many organizations that change, it's often those who oppose implementation who are the ones who need the belief system the most. Uncomfortable with change in general, they will resist any approach that requires them to modify their attitudes and behaviors, even though that's exactly what they need to do in order to cope with change better.

What can you do to promote universal acceptance of this change-management tool? The best strategy is to anticipate potentially negative reactions and plan ways to overcome them. While the approach is unlikely to work with managers who feel they're being forced to apply it, most will welcome it if they're convinced of its merits and understand what it can do for them personally.

Applying the belief system itself may help you to change the minds of these resisters. How? By strengthening their B-1, B-2, and B-3 beliefs regarding the approach. For example, whenever managers voice objections to implementing the belief system with their teams, show them that they'll gain a practical tool and new skills for managing change (B-1), demonstrate how much more effective they can be in their jobs when they work to manage change (B-2), and outline the desirable results they can achieve by using the approach (B-3).

Lesson 3

Implement at multiple levels simultaneously.

We have explained cascading and the importance of implementing the belief system approach at all levels of an organization in change (see Chapters 7 and 8). Within the Eastern Region, cascading was carried out in a top-down manner. One-on-ones were conducted first between the Sales Vice President and his direct reports, then between branch managers and sales managers, and finally between sales managers and the sales representatives who make up their teams. There are clear advantages to cascading in this way: It promotes increased management buy-in to the belief system process and makes sure that managers understand their new roles and responsibilities before they conduct one-on-one sessions with their subordinates. There are also disadvantages however: Cascading from one organizational level to the next slows down the implementation process considerably and may deny people at lower levels access to the approach when they need it most.

Most organizations do not have the luxury of waiting six months to a year before seeing the results that the belief system can produce. For them, a simultaneous approach may be a more practical way to cascade. Though this means that some managers may participate in application sessions with their direct reports before they've had a chance to meet one on one with *their* boss, this does not diminish the power of the approach significantly, and it may help organizations to achieve positive results earlier in the change process.

Lesson 4

Focus on those areas where you'll do the most good.

For any number of reasons, organizations may not be able to implement the belief system at multiple levels simultaneously. There may be logistical obstacles that prevent them from cascading the approach in this way, or they may face time or budgetary constraints that force them to implement the approach in a more progressive fashion. In these cases, leaders typically ask where they should start when implementing the belief system. Common sense applies: Implement the approach first in those areas where it will do the most good. These include the following:

Front-Line Areas

This is where the people work who make your product or service and interact directly with your customers, so it's critical that they accept the change imperative, get on with the change initiatives, and get the help they need to adopt new practices and adjust to a new work environment. When change fails to have the desired effect on your front lines, it's unlikely to produce the results that you expect or hope for organizationwide.

Strategic Areas

In every organization there are functions or departments that are essential to customer satisfaction and achieving strategic goals. These are the areas where you should focus your improvement efforts. In a high-tech company, these strategic areas may include R&D and marketing. In an insurance firm, sales and claim-processing functions may be the areas to target first.

Problem Areas

It also helps to implement the approach quickly in those areas where change is of a greater magnitude than in other parts of the organization, where manager–employee relationships are new or problematic, or where people are especially resistant to change. By working to implement in problem areas first, you eliminate potential obstacles to change from the start and increase your chances of long-term success.

Lesson 5

Provide the tools that people need to change.

One of the most important ways the belief system works to improve motivation during change is by helping to identify what people need in order to change. In general, employees and managers are more willing to change if they know they'll get the resources and support that will make it possible for them to do it. These tools may take a variety of forms: cross-training, classroom instruction, coaching, or mentoring. But it must also include patience and a tolerance for failure. People need to feel that the expectations established for them are realistic, that they'll have enough time to learn what they must in order to change successfully, and that they won't be punished for making mistakes as they work to improve.

Though many organizations limit the resources they allocate for change, it's better to provide too much support than too little. And the best organizations go to considerable lengths to make sure their people get all the help they need. When NationsBank reengineered the division that handles its letter-of-credit operations, for example, two of the most experienced employees in its Atlanta location were taken off their jobs and designated as full-time trainers. Using a program that they developed, they offered instruction to coworkers in redesigned jobs that included self-taught manuals, case studies, and lab work.[1]

The support you provide doesn't have to be this formal or systematic, as long as it works to reassure employees and assist them as they change. Within the Eastern Region of Middle Markets, this was accomplished in part through a greater emphasis on coaching, to which managers are now expected to allot 40 percent of their time. Though managers sometimes had to be reminded of their new coaching responsibilities, the increased personal attention that employees received played a key role in helping them to successfully work through change-related issues.

Lesson 6

Deal swiftly with individuals who aren't willing to change.

The belief system approach gives leaders the opportunity to identify early those who will resist the change and those who won't be able to perform the way the change requires. But leaders are not always able to act on this information. They may feel uncomfortable in making termination decisions or feel bound by past practices or cultural traditions to delay taking such drastic measures.

It's counterproductive for organizations to adopt a wait-and-see attitude whenever they encounter resistance to change. By holding on to managers or employees who may never accept change, they reduce their chances of making change succeed and run the risk of "infecting" those who are motivated to change with their coworkers' negative attitudes.

This was one of the most important, though difficult, lessons learned by the leaders of the Eastern Region. Operating in a culture where turnover had historically been low, they weren't used to acting swiftly in matters of termination, and it wasn't easy for them to let people go. But they soon learned that dealing quickly and decisively with those who resist change is essential to developing a team with the proper mindset and to moving forward with the resolve and commitment that organizational change requires.

Lesson 7

Use trained facilitators when conducting one-on-one sessions.

We believe that the facilitator is a critical component of the belief system approach and is crucial to the success of the one-on-one sessions. As the leaders of the Eastern Region learned, when a facilitator is used to supervise these meetings, they usually achieve the two purposes they're designed to accomplish: to get employees involved in solving their own motivation and performance problems, and to improve working relationships between managers and employees.

When properly trained, the facilitator helps participants to feel more comfortable during their session, encourages them to open up and talk frankly, and guides the discussion toward critical issues. In many organizations, the facilitator also plays a role of "change agent" for the managers and employees that he or she works with. The facilitator may provide assistance in helping participants to prepare for their session, for example, or call participants between sessions to evaluate the progress they're making.

During the implementation of the belief system in the Eastern Region, the facilitator used in one-on-one sessions was the originator of the approach and coauthor of this book, Thad Green. But organizations can train their own facilitators to serve the same function. All that's required is a thorough understanding of the concepts and methodology of the belief system approach and the interpersonal skills needed to facilitate productive discussions, mediate conflicts, and promote mutual understanding.

Lesson 8

Establish priorities for your To Do list.

Every one-on-one session results in To Do lists: action plans based on commitments that the manager and employee each make to the other. For change to take place, both parties must fulfill these commitments, and the follow-up session held six months later is conducted primarily to determine how well managers and employees live up to their promises.

Is it realistic to expect participants to accomplish every item on their list? For the majority of employees, the answer is yes. Typically, each participant leaves the session with a To Do list of about five items, so most employees are able to make considerable progress on their commitments in the six-month period between their initial one-on-one session and their follow-up session.

For many managers, however, prioritizing is often essential because their participation in multiple sessions may result in a compiled To Do list that's substantial. A manager who conducts one-on-one sessions with eight direct reports, for example, could conceivably end up with a To Do list of forty items or more, though in most cases these lists are shorter because of overlap in the issues that employees bring up with any one manager.

Even with a relatively manageable list of ten to twelve items, managers should prioritize to (1) make sure they work on the most critical issues that affect their organization and their relationships with employees, and (2) avoid feelings of being overwhelmed. Managers who don't prioritize may experience serious B-1 problems ("I'll never be able to do all that") or B-3 problems ("Even if I get the outcomes I want, it's not worth all the effort I have to put into it"). A practical prioritizing strategy for managers is to identify the five most important issues to work on first, then revisit your To Do list to determine where you need to focus your improvement efforts next.

Lesson 9

Continually reinforce new attitudes and practices.

In most organizations that apply it, the belief system becomes a new way of managing that dramatically alters and improves relationships at work. The one-on-one meetings that are central to the approach become important opportunities for productive discussions that both managers and employees come to rely on. Managers can better communicate objectives and expectations, while employees can express feelings and concerns and surface problems.

In some cases, the language of the approach becomes widely adopted and is assimilated into an organization's culture, serving as a useful means to defuse emotionally charged situations or help individuals to save face. For example, instead of admitting ignorance by saying, "I just don't understand what you mean when you talk about the marginal cost method of pricing," an employee can say without embarrassment, "I have a B-1 problem with marginal cost pricing."

As with any improvement strategy, however, the gains you make by using this approach won't be sustained unless you continually reinforce the new attitudes and practices that it promotes. Otherwise, the belief system becomes just another "program of the month," a one-shot opportunity to induce change, but with no long-term impact. People may change at first, but then they slip back into old behaviors and your benefits are short lived. This was the lament of one Eastern Region manager who felt his team hadn't applied the belief system consistently enough. "We still have to stop and think to use it," he said in an interview about six months after the approach was introduced. "Consequently, our boss has reverted back to her old ways, and we've let her."

There are several steps you can take to ensure the ongoing effectiveness of the belief system:

1. Adhere to a strict schedule of follow-up sessions every six months. This will help you to incorporate the approach as an integral component of your performance-management system.
2. Periodically conduct half-day learning sessions that provide a more in-depth understanding of the belief system. This helps to remind your people of the rationale for the approach and its concepts and objectives.
3. Hold special meetings to evaluate the approach and the results you've achieved. This builds ongoing support for using the approach and gives people the opportunity to contribute their ideas on how it can be implemented more effectively.

Lesson 10

Integrate change-management initiatives.

Every large-scale transformation incorporates a multitude of change strategies. No organization can count on just one approach to bring about renewal and meet radically new objectives. Leaders increase their chances of failure, in fact, when they pin their hopes for success on a single change-management tool. This is not to suggest that the belief system is no better than other improvement strategies, nor does it weaken our endorsement for the approach. On the contrary, one of the reasons why we believe the belief system works so well is that it can be integrated easily with a variety of change-management initiatives and usually enhances their effectiveness.

In the Eastern Region of Middle Markets, for example, at least a dozen strategies were deployed to bring about structural and cultural change, including the new financial model, MaxPace, and "Where's Waldo?" When implementing each strategy, managers relied on the belief system—and on its ability to flush out problems and achieve consensus—to ensure understanding of what needed to be done, overcome resistance, and identify where help had to be provided to bring about the expected change.

Organizational leaders today have numerous change methods at their disposal, from TQM and reengineering to self-directed and high-performance teams. The belief system is not intended as a substitute for these improvement strategies, but, rather, as a tool that can be applied to expedite their acceptance and implementation. Therefore, we encourage leaders to integrate this approach with their other change initiatives to increase the power and effectiveness of whatever change formula they choose.

Lesson 11

Measure your progress and communicate results.

Whenever people are asked to change, they have a right to know what they've accomplished and whether their efforts are leading to success. To build support for change and maintain momentum, every organization in transition must develop measures to track the outcomes of its change initiatives and communicate results.

This advice holds true for the belief system as for any other improvement strategy. Managers and employees must invest a considerable amount of time and energy in this approach, so it's reasonable for them to expect reliable feedback on their participation—that is, regular and objective assessments of what they've achieved. In the Eastern Region, this feedback was based on several quantitative measures, including leadership surveys and the AT&T Opinion Survey, the results of which were communicated widely throughout the organization (see Chapter 13).

Providing this information serves a dual purpose. Not only does it satisfy the need that people have to see the results of their efforts, it also increases motivation and promotes continued progress. When people have the opportunity to evaluate their achievements and feel good about them, they usually want to build on early successes and move ahead to accomplish more.

Lesson 12

Hold people accountable for their commitment to improve.

One of the chief benefits of the belief system is the clarity that it brings to motivation and performance issues at work. With this approach, managers and employees gain greater insight into problems they face in their jobs and with each other, how these problems came about, and what can be done to solve them. But this approach won't work if those who participate are not held accountable for the commitments they make as they work through the process. Without accountability at every level, managers and employees will not assume responsibility for their improvement, nor will they make the effort to change in the ways that are needed for organizational success.

The belief system approach incorporates elements that encourage accountability, such as team meetings, To Do lists, and follow-up sessions. But organizations can and must do more, by working to establish a culture of accountability and by taking decisive action whenever commitments are not met. Both managers and employees must be made to realize that their promises to improve are the foundation on which organizational change takes place.

By taking these steps, organizations can maximize the power of the belief system approach where it has the greatest impact: within each individual. This generates a ripple effect that produces important benefits organizationwide. When one person changes by adopting new attitudes and behaviors, others inevitably change too, as BCS leaders learned. The cumulative power of individual change is the key to successful organizational change.

Finally, it should also be remembered that no change-management technique or leadership tool can substitute for sound, principled, and compassionate management. But even the most principled and compassionate managers sometimes need help and guidance. Managing people is far more difficult than managing processes or money or systems, because managing people is really about winning their hearts and their minds.

Tips for Implementing the Change Model

1. Establish the optimal time for implementation.
2. Maximize your benefits through increased participation.
3. Implement at multiple levels simultaneously.
4. Focus on those areas where you'll do the most good.
5. Provide the support that people need to change.
6. Deal swiftly with those who aren't willing to change.
7. Use trained facilitators in one-on-one sessions.
8. Establish priorities for your To Do list.
9. Continually reinforce new attitudes and practices.
10. Integrate change-management initiatives.
11. Measure progress and communicate results.
12. Hold people accountable for their commitment to improve.

NOTE

1. Robert Janson, Dennis Attenello, John A. Uzzi, *Reengineering for Results: A Step-by-Step Guide* (Quality Resources, New York, 1995), 172.

Annotated Bibliography

Feather, Norman T., ed. *Expectations and Actions: Expectancy-Value Models in Psychology.* Hillsdale, N.J.: Lawrence Erlbaum Associates, 1982. Analyzing the evolution of expectancy theory over a twenty-year period, this book examines the strengths and weaknesses of the approach as a psychological model and shows how it has been applied by various thinkers to explain human behavior at work. Expectancy theory is seen as a theoretical advance beyond the simple stimulus-response interpretation of human behavior, one that sees people as active processors of information who consult their own conceptual or cognitive maps before taking action.

Green, Thad B. *Performance and Motivation Strategies for Today's Workforce: A Guide to Expectancy Theory Applications.* Westport, Conn.: Quorum Books, 1992. This book presents the first application model that gives practical value to the expectancy theory of motivation, providing techniques and tools managers can use to identify, diagnose, and solve motivation problems at work. Included are specific guidelines on what managers should say and do to determine the causes of individual motivation problems, effective ways to resolve problems in the early stages before they get out of hand, and a framework for involving employees in resolving their own motivation and performance problems.

Lawler, Edward E. *Motivation in Work Organizations.* Monterey, Calif.: Brooks/ Cole, 1973. Dealing extensively with both theory and practice, this book was written for students of organizational behavior as well as for managers who must deal with the day-to-day motivation problems that occur at work. Discussing various influences on motivation and performance—including job design, leadership style, and pay systems—Lawler claims that the ability to analyze work situations from a motivational perspective is critical for managers if they are to effectively resolve the many complex performance problems they confront on the job.

Lawler, Edward E. *Pay and Organizational Effectiveness: A Psychological View.* New York: McGraw-Hill, 1971. This book addresses some fundamental questions that deal with human behavior in work organizations, particularly the role of monetary compensation and the impact of pay administration on individual and organizational effectiveness. After analyzing various theories of motivation, Lawler focuses on the psychological problems that arise when money is used to pay people for their work, discusses why and when money operates to motivate workers, and analyzes the effects of pay secrecy and pay equity on group performance.

Nadler, David, Robert B. Shaw, A. Elise Walton, and Associates. *Discontinuous Change: Leading Organizational Transformation.* San Francisco: Jossey-Bass, 1995. Written by members of the Delta Consulting Group, this book is a comprehensive handbook for change leaders that outlines the primary challenges organizations face when they undertake large-scale change. Included are essays on transforming culture, sustaining change, and the fundamentals of change management, as well as interviews with executives who initiated major change efforts, including Bob Allen of AT&T and Jamie Houghton of Corning.

University of Michigan Survey Research Center. *Michigan Organizational Assessment Package: Progress Report II.* Ann Arbor: University of Michigan Institute for Social Research, 1975. Drawing on the work of Victor Vroom and Edward Lawler, the Michigan Assessment of Organizations (MAO), reproduced in this report, is a broad-gauged employee attitude survey that can be adapted to different work settings and used to measure employee attitudes and feelings about a wide variety of organizational issues. Consisting of ten standardized modules, the MAO includes about 350 items that address such areas as job satisfaction, leadership style, work motivation, performance outcomes, and employee beliefs and values.

Vroom, Victor H. *Motivation in Management.* New York: American Foundation for Management Research, 1965. This study was one of the first to focus on the interplay between motives and work among managers and summarizes existing research on the motivational patterns that distinguish managers from hourly workers and other occupational groups. Some of the major issues discussed include how the desires of managers differ from those of other members of the labor force, what motivational differences exist among levels of management in various fields, and the effects of management behavior on the job satisfaction and performance of subordinates.

Vroom, Victor H. *Work and Motivation*. New York: John Wiley & Sons, 1964. In this landmark book in organizational psychology, Vroom broke new ground by integrating the work of hundreds of researchers to present a new conceptual model of workplace behavior. Joining theory with empirical research, Vroom examines a variety of issues related to work and human behavior, including occupational choice, work satisfaction, and the role of motivation in work performance. (The 1994 edition, published by Jossey-Bass, includes a new introduction by the author.)

Weisbord, Marvin R. *Productive Workplaces: Organizing and Managing for Dignity, Meaning, and Community*. San Francisco: Jossey-Bass, 1987. This book provides a comprehensive history of the theories of work motivation and organizational development, beginning with the revolutionary work of Frederick Taylor, the so-called "father of scientific management." Weisbord discusses the ideas of seminal thinkers in this field, including Kurt Lewin, Douglas McGregor, Rensis Likert, and Frederick Herzberg, and shows how practitioners have used their ideas to transform work organizations and create more productive and more satisfying jobs for people.

Woodward, Harry and Steve Buchholz. *Aftershock: Helping People Through Corporate Change*. New York: John Wiley & Sons, 1987. This book was one of the first to deal with the often-overlooked human side of corporate change, providing an in-depth examination of the breakdown in morale that often accompanies mergers, reengineering efforts, and restructurings. Using research conducted by William Bridges, the book offers recommendations to managers for dealing with what they say are four common emotional reactions to large-scale change: disengagement, disidentification, disorientation, and disenchantment.

Index

Communication, value of, 34–35
Confidence: defined, 16; rating
scales, 24, 70–71, 76
Confidence problems, 17, 19, 26–27;
anticipating, 61; causes, 26;
diagnosing, 35–38; solving, 38
Confusion, 6, 127–128
Culture: change, 58–59; transformations, 60; turnarounds, 59–60

Decision making, 68–69, 72–73
Disappointment, 6
Discomfort, 6

Effort, 16
Emotions, 5–7, 124–125; associated
with problems, 17; impact on
change, 5–7, 110–111; impact on
teams, 47–48; managers and, 7–8;
organizations in change, profile
of, 125–28; run amok, 96–97;
turnarounds, 158; upheaval, 110–
111
Employee opinion, 104–105, 165–167
Excitment, 6
Execution, focusing on, 190–191
Expectancy theory, 19–20
Expectations, 100, 116; establishing,
143–145

Fear, 6
Financial modeling, 119
Follow-up session, 92–93

Hard-to-solve problems, 153–155
Hope, 6

Identity, 127–128
Image, 126–127
Implementation: of the belief system
at multiple levels, 93; strategies
for successful, 191–200
Incentive programs, 16–18
Incentives, 16–17
Individuals: leading to change, 33–
44; managing to 144–145
Insecurity, 6, 125–126

Job mismatches, 154–155

Learning, 74–77; through repetition,
148

Management style, 51, 149–152;
matching to employee needs, 150–
151
Managing change. *See* Change
MaxPACE, 117–118
Money, motivating power of, 156–
158
Motivation: conditions for, 11;
payoff, 12; preconditions, 20;
types of problems, 17, 35; uncovering problems, 18–23; what
motivates most people, 157
Motivation problems: causes and
solutions, 23–29; uncovering, 18–
23

One-on-one sessions, 83–92; career-
altering, 140; conducting, 89–92;
diagnostic tools, 85–89; employee
role, 84–85; implementing, 138–
142; manager role, 84–85; relation-
ship-altering, 140–142
Organizational analysis, 34; tools for,
60–65; using the belief system for,
63
Outcomes, 16

Panic, 127–128
Performance, 16
Performance problems, predicting,
61
Planning, 119–120
Positive reinforcement, value of, 73–
74
Preferred motivation environment,
86–89

Rating scales, 24–25, 70–71, 75–76
Relationships, 101–102
Results, 104–106, 145–146; bottom-
line, 160–162; employee opinion
survey, 165–167; leadership

ABOUT THE AUTHORS

Thad B. Green is a management consultant specializing in the people problems associated with organizational change. Founder and principal of The Belief System Institute, a center for the advancement of motivation and performance based in Atlanta, Georgia, Dr. Green has taught management at the University of Georgia, Auburn University, Mississippi State University, and Emory University. Among his present and former clients are corporations such as AT&T, Lucent Technologies, and Metropolitan Life Insurance. He is author or coauthor of more than 11 books, including three published by Quorum: *Performance and Motivation Strategies for Today's Workforce* (1992), *Developing and Leading the Sales Organization* (1998), and *Breaking the Barrier to Upward Communications* (1999, with Jay T. Knippen).

Raymond T. Butkus worked for AT&T for many years in various management and executive positions. In his most recent assignment he served as Sales Vice President in AT&T's Business Communications Services Division, where he led a 1000-member group selling communications services to middle-market companies throughout the Northeast. He is author of numerous articles on sales management, telecommunications, and marketing. He is currently Vice President and General Manager for Intelliquest, a New York City firm.